GROWTH IS DEAD: NOW WHAT?

Growth Is Dead: Now What?
Law firms on the brink

BRUCE MACEWEN

FOREWORD BY PETER J. KALIS

Adam Smith, Esq.®
New York
2013

Published by Adam Smith, Esq., LLC
305 West 98th Street
New York, New York 10025
USA

Second Printing

Library of Congress Cataloging-in-Publication Data is available
ISBN 978-1481896047

Growth Is Dead was originally published
in twelve online installments
on AdamSmithEsq.com during the fall of 2012.

The version you are reading here is identical except for minor
technical adaptations.

Composed and published at New York, New York.

Printed in the United States of America

Cover design by faucethead creative

WHAT PEOPLE ARE SAYING

"I read all 12 installments of your series with great inter-
est...twice. This is an extraordinary body of work that reflects
enormous insight and ought to be required reading by managing partners of law firms and professional services organizations. You do a very effective job of challenging the status quo
and your series is a much-needed wake up call for our profession. As always, I plan to share many of your insights with
my partners. And I plan to cogitate over many of your pro-
posed initiatives."

— Brad Karp, Chair of the Firm, Paul Weiss

A high-profile law-firm consultant offers a grim prognosis,
and advice, for the upper echelons of the legal profession.
Debut author MacEwen — the president of consultancy Adam
Smith, Esq., a former securities lawyer and a writer of numerous articles on economic and strategic issues facing large, sophisticated law firms — warns in this brief, to-the-point volume that top-grossing firms must either adapt to the post-2008
economic reset or risk extinction.
He addresses a range of problems, such as the lack of growth
in client demand, a surplus of highly paid partners doing too
little and junior lawyers with unrealistic career expectations,
cost-cutting globalization, ever-evolving technology that
drives fewer to do more, and emboldened clients demanding
lower legal fees.

The overriding question, MacEwen says, is whether these be-leaguered law firms will be self-aware enough to reinvent themselves in the face of vastly altered economic realities. Or, like Herman Melville's scrivener Bartleby, will they simply prefer not to? MacEwen writes that lawyers' natural aversion to failure could lead to trouble when trial-and-error reinvention is the order of the day.

"I submit that our rigid intolerance for failure is so extreme and ultimately perverse that it disables us from being capable of smart decision making," he declares. The author's writing style is straightforward, engaging, and urbane yet informal and never recondite.

— *Kirkus Reviews*

CONTENTS

FOREWORD

By
Peter J. Kalis*

The global pandemic known as Legal Complexity ought to present the best of times for the modern law firm. Consider:

1. Globalization – the movement of people, products, commodities, services, capital, and ideas across national borders -- paradoxically enhances rather than diminishes the importance of sovereignty and national legal systems. Simply put, clients need advice on this side of the border, on the other side of the border and on how to cross the border legally and efficiently.

2. The ratchet-like interventions into private markets by governments around the world require regulatory and legislative solutions for enterprises intent upon staying in business – more so if they wish to grow their businesses and prosper. These governmental interventions are partly attributable to partisan impulse but more fundamentally to the growing body of knowledge upon which those charged with public missions can reasonably ground their actions. We now know more, to cite a few examples, about human activities that affect the climate or about the triggers for sub-clinical disease processes or about the global interdependence of financial markets. Of course legislators and regulators must act. Not always wisely, to be sure, but their work product grows daily.

3. What of the legal demands of an innovation-driven economy? The daily exploits of the technology sector are well reported – from telecommunications to information solutions to robotics to biotechnology and more. But let's not forget traditional, smokestack industries in which innovations dictate whether razor-thin margins will be maintained. The creation and protection of intellectual property are paramount among the modern enterprise's legal challenges.

Nevertheless, these are decidedly not the best of times for "Big Law" or the legal industry generally. The perpetually robust growth in law firm financial metrics that characterized recent decades is missing in action -- presumed to be a battlefield casualty in the (so far) Five Year War precipitated by the demise of those fallen Archdukes of modern capitalism, Bear Stearns and Lehman. There are reverberations throughout the legal industry. Fewer young people are choosing law as a career; morale in law firms is said to be low; lifestyle aspirations of many law partners and associates have been frustrated. In short, the parallel universe of Big Law has been sucked into the black hole known as Reality.

What's going on here? For the answer to this and other questions fundamental to the economics of the legal industry, we turn time and again to Bruce MacEwen, whose 12-part series "Growth is Dead" in *AdamSmithEsq.com* is so usefully presented in this volume. Who else but Bruce would have introduced his legal industry readers – nearly two years before "Growth is Dead" incepted -- to the work of Reinhart and Rogoff (*This Time Is Different: Eight Centuries of Financial Folly*), the splendid study alerting us that, when viewed against the sweep of history, the recessionary conditions following the Global Financial Crisis would be uncharacteristically long. By this measure, the legal industry and its clients have more miles to go before we can say confidently that better times are ahead.

For Bruce, however, Reinhart and Rogoff, while undoubtedly offering part of the explanation for the lethargy in legal markets, perhaps provide too easy an answer because their admirable study suggests for law firms a degree not of fatalism but of complacency disguised as patience. Bruce – sorry, readers, for the following visual but it's how Bruce's mind works -- tenaciously scrapes away that scab and dives into the wound to see what besides "financial folly" is there.

Plenty, as it turns out. Bruce sees in the legal marketplace the confluence of several interrelated phenomena that followed upon the Global Financial Crisis: pricing pressures; excess capacity; the proliferation of career tracks; unrealistic partner expectations; heightened partner mobility; and the enlarged significance of strategic planning in law firm success.

OK, fair enough. Times are tough, and strategic positioning can be a key to survival. All of this is quite interesting, of course, but surficial. What's beneath the surface? Bruce does not disappoint, as there he finds the legal industry perched precariously at the intersection of globalization and technological advancement and concludes that law firms either embrace this new reality or face uncertain and probably unpleasant consequences.

Drawing upon lessons learned in industries far afield from law, Bruce pushes hard for a new legal culture – one that embraces a long-term view, a client-oriented innovation model, an ethos grounded in creative experimentation and simplicity. How to achieve this new culture? That you will find in the following pages. Not for a novitiate to profess.

At the risk of eliciting Bruce's disapproval, I will end by disputing a core proposition he advances. Bruce maintains that *AdamSmithEsq.com* "is an inquiry into the economics of law firms." True enough, I suppose, just as it is true that Michelangelo did some interesting things with pigments on the ceiling of the Sistine Chapel. But Bruce is about more than supply and demand. He is really about promoting fundamental, idea-driven change in the legal culture. His whip is the English language, and the snap comes from his deep insights not only into law and economics but also into cognate disciplines such as psychology, history, organizational theory and, for lack of a better term, good old human nature. Make no mistake about it. Bruce is a cultural radical – as was his 18th Century namesake Adam Smith -- and we're all the better for it.

---

*Chairman and Global Managing Partner, K&L Gates LLP.

1: SETTING THE STAGE

If you believe the structural environment for BigLaw hasn't fundamentally changed since 2008, the book in your hands is not for you. (I would also have to ask, from a mystified perspective and in the kindest of ways, if you're paying attention?)

Call it the Great Recession, the Great Reset (my favorite), or whatever, the world palpably shook in September 2008 and the repercussions are still very much with us.

Herewith, then, the first chapter of Growth is Dead.

In this chapter, we'll be talking about pricing pressures. Future chapters will address the following, and more:

- Excess capacity
- The proliferation of career tracks
- Partner expectations
- Lateral partner mobility
- And the critical role of truly strategic thinking

Yes, many of these topics are deeply interconnected. For example, pricing pressure and excess capacity (see: Microeconomics 101), or partner expectations and lateral partner mobility, but I think they're sufficiently distinguishable to be worth analyzing in separate chapters.

I look forward to your thoughts, suggestions, and comments—and if there are one or more topics you'd like me to add to the list, please suggest them in an email to me.

First a bit of background

Let's begin by rehearsing some baseline, but critical, data. If we don't all agree at the outset on some of the patient's symptoms, we have no prayer of agreeing on a diagnosis.

I have borrowed heavily in what follows from the Hildebrandt/Citi Private Bank 2012 Client Advisory, since it has the following virtues: (a) it's as current as anything available; (b) its sources are actual firm financials, not wistful beauty-contest aspirations; and (c) it's publicly available so open to critique and correction.

Let's start with an overview of the growth, or decline, in key financials comparing the period immediately before the meltdown with the period immediately after.

Impact of the Market Downturn

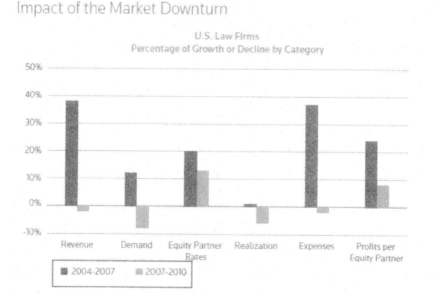

If you want to deny things have changed, you would point to Equity Partner Rates and PPEP, but for purposes of this discussion I disagree. The time series I would call out are Revenue, Demand and Realization – all down. I focus on those three series because equity partner rates and PPEP are internal financial reports essentially under the control of firms (at least in the short run, and three years still qualifies as the short run). The ones I prefer to focus on are creatures of the market and reflect market forces.

Lest you protest that partner rates being up displays a "healthy" trend, let's look more closely at realization.

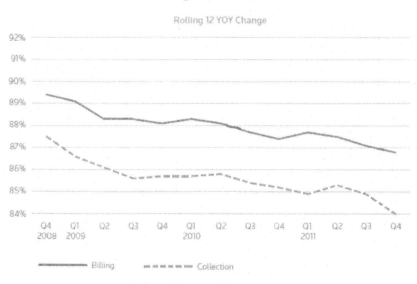

Collected Realization Rate against Standard: All Firms

Any way you want to look at it, this tells a dramatic and – if you're rooting for BigLaw, alarming – story. By the way, the definition of "collected realization rate against standard" is the percentage of work "performed at a firm's standard rates that is actually billed to and collected from clients."

We are collecting, industry-wide, less than 85 cents on the dollar. Imagine another industry that (de facto) gave its average customer a 15% discount day in and day out. We would immediately, and correctly, leap to the conclusion that one or both of two things are true about that industry: It's charging too much or it's delivering too little.

Remember this is an average: Are you thinking that you and your firm are in the blessed minority for whom this isn't true? If that's what you're thinking (and if it's honest to God true that your firm is healthily above these lines), then bully for you.

But, folks, for every reader knocking on wood that their firm is above these lines, there is, statistically speaking, another reader whose firm is below these lines.

I've written recently that I believe never before have averages been so misleading, and I would like to reaffirm it here for the record.

We'll get to why strategy, and differentiation, matter more than ever, but that's towards the end of this series. For now we're talking about the industry writ large.

Pricing Pressures

Simply put, clients are pushing back as never before. Among other things, they are:

- serious, for the first time, about alternative fee arrangements, caps and blended rates, rate freezes, and so on

- strongly resisting—even refusing—paying for junior associates
- requiring that major segments of a matter, be it litigation or transactional, be handled by LPOs, staff/contract/temp lawyers, or anything other than full-time partner-track associates.

Don't take my word for it. Here are two remarks managing partners have made to me in the past few months:

- "What we used to assign a dozen associates to now only takes four" and
- "Raising rates? No problem; piece of cake. But raise rates 5% and realization drops 6%."

We also see what I call "suicidal pricing" in response to RFPs. These are bids—from name-brand firms, mind you—that are so breathtakingly low one wonders how they could possibly make any money. The short answer is they can't. These bids come in 5, 10, 20, 40% under what my clients think would be reasonable for the matter. But in a desperate and/or deluded attempt to keep the factory whirring away, such bids are calculated and submitted in the full light of day.

Rarely do I adopt this posture, but permit me to prostrate myself in front of you and beg your firm not to engage in suicidal pricing. Why not?

- The immediate result is that you will, by hypothesis, lose money on the deal. Best avoided.
- A medium-term result is that you will, as department stores succeeded in doing to the industry's systematic ruination, train your clients never to purchase services from you except when you offer them drastically discounted: "40% off sale."

• The final and long-term result is that you have single-handedly devalued what your firm can offer in the eyes of your clients. Kiss goodbye to any fantasy of aspiring to the "high value, price-insensitive work" that everyone and their brother thinks is their firm's rightful entitlement. The psychology is not obscure: If you [clearly] don't much value what you do, why should I?

Finally, I did a tour of duty as an inhouse counsel (here in New York at then-Morgan Stanley/Dean Witter) and I have news for you: Good clients do not want trusted law firms to lose money. They really don't. They want you around for the long run.

Part of achieving that, being around for the long run, will involve conquering the pricing pressure dragon. Not every firm will.

2: EXCESS CAPACITY

Welcome to the second chapter of "Growth is Dead:" Our topic for today is excess capacity. Let's start with overall supply of new lawyers, which is the font of everything else. Thanks to the redoubtable Prof. Paul Campos (University of Colorado Law), we have a comprehensive summary of a combination of the best available numbers from the US Bureau of Labor Statistics and the American Bar Association, we learn that:

Between 2010 and 2020, the US economy will produce 218,800 job openings for lawyers and judicial clerks, or a little under 22,000 per year

These statistics include filling the slots of retirees and other job force departures as well as new job openings

They're based on historically "normal" 10-year business cycles, so if you believe we're in a long-term and slow employment recovery, they could be overestimates

US law schools granted 44,004 JDs in 2010, which rose slightly to 44,258 in 2011 and 44,495 in 2012

As they say, "do the math:" 132,757 new JDs in 3 years would fill 61% of all available lawyer jobs for the next decade

And there's no obvious end in sight; law schools are cash cows for their universities (or themselves, if unaffiliated) and no individual school has an incentive to cut enrollment barring some highly improbable pact surmounting the "collective action" psychological and economic barrier. (Yes, some pathbreaking schools such as UC Hastings/SF, under the leadership of Frank Wu, are breaking from the pack, but they're countable on the fingers of one hand.)

Graphically, it looks like this — EVERY YEAR FOR THE NEXT 10 YEARS:

Legal Sector Employment: 2010—2020

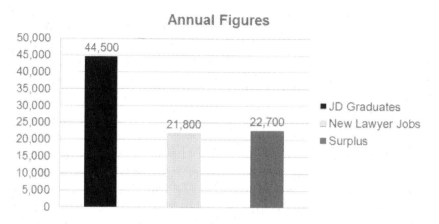

Annual Figures

Source: Bureau of Labor Statistics, ABA

The next step is to examine the supply/demand landscape more specifically for BigLaw. Here, NALP always has the most comprehensive and thorough statistics. From their "Perspectives on Fall 2011 Law Student Recruiting" and from a presentation Jim Leipold (NALP Executive Director) delivered in New York earlier this year:

"Law firms continue to bring in small summer classes, barely increasing class size from recession-era lows."

Structural changes include greater competition from LPOs and offshore firms

Lawyer jobs increasingly are being lost to technology

Compared to pre-recession numbers, there are significantly fewer private practice jobs-down by 10% just from 2010 to 2011

With a 20% drop in average salaries

Leading to higher law graduate un- and underemployment

Fewer law graduates overall are working as lawyers

New grads are competing with displaced lawyers

Salaries for new grads actually employed as lawyers - be the measure median, mean, or "adjusted mean" (a NALP statistic) are down about 12% IN ONE YEAR.

****

Now, all this has addressed the macro environment for lawyers in general and BigLaw in particular. But in microeconomics, "excess capacity" has a slightly different—and more pointed—meaning as applied to specific firms within a pertinent market segment, and it's to that I now wish to turn. Notice I said "pertinent market segment." I would argue that the market for BigLaw services (or SophisticatedLaw services, perhaps more accurately) is in all ways that matter a market segment distinct from US national economic demand for "lawyers" in general or legal services in general. From that perspective it actually doesn't matter much to BigLaw whether there's a pervasive oversupply of lawyers in the 50 States; it matters whether BigLaw itself has excess capacity. And does it ever. Managing Partners tell me this, other consultants are telling this to the media, and it seems universally recognized. We have:

too many associates given what clients are willing to pay for

too many of-counsel and non-equity partners, who are clogging the advancement pipeline for those below them, and

in many firms, too many equity partners, if judged on rigorous performance criteria (or if simply judged on the number of equity partners Firm X can support at the PPEP to which it has become accustomed).

THIS IS NOT THOSE PEOPLE'S FAULT. It's the result of the historic path our industry has taken over the past 30 or so years, growing like clockwork at high single-digit rates, and never before September 2008 having experienced a sustained, systemic, enduring, macroeconomic downward shift in demand for our services. Don't take my word for it. Here are the latest numbers from the Citi/Hildebrandt 2012 Client Advisory on demand "growth" (or lack thereof, obviously) by key practice areas:

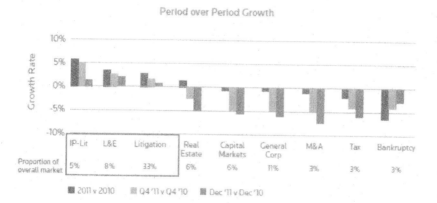

Here's what stands out to me:

Pretty much across the board, demand is continuing to fall:

Dec '11 vs. Dec '10 is the worst time series (black right-hand bars in each triplet)

Q4 '11 v. Q4 '10 is the second-worst time series (medium grey middle bars), and

2011 v 2010 is the "healthiest" series (left hand dark grey bars)

The two areas growing fastest—IP litigation and labor & employment—together make up only 13% of law firm revenue, while the six shrinking segments account for 32% of revenue (note that the practice areas displayed account only for about 75% of total revenue, presumably because displaying them all would require more detail than would be useful).

In terms of excess capacity, falling demand is a classic, and usually the #1, driving component. After all, firms don't usually overhire recklessly or build new factories before they have customers, so purposefully creating excess supply is extremely rare and I would hazard never intended. Now let's turn to "productivity" (for another day is the debate over whether the word "productivity" is an inapt, if not distorting and insulting, name for gross billable hours, but everyone seems to know what it means and we will, for today, stick with it):

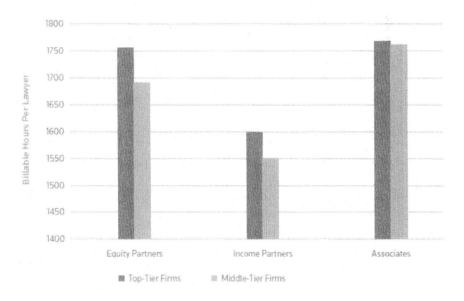

Average Annual Productivity by Timekeeper (2001-2010)

We have to look at this in conjunction with the evolving composition of timekeepers to gather the full story. Here's that data:

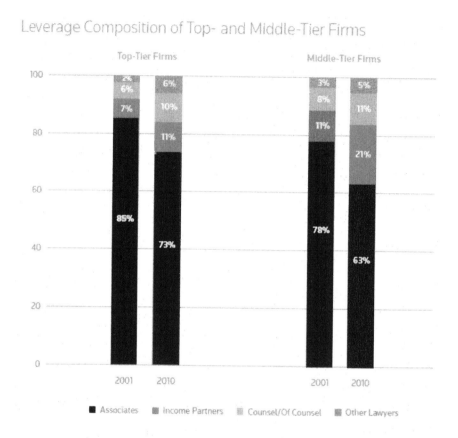

Leverage Composition of Top- and Middle-Tier Firms

Putting these two charts together, here's what we've been doing to ourselves: We have systematically increased our reliance on the most expensive, least productive cohort of our lawyers. This is not the behavior of rational firms doing all they can to increase their value to clients.

(Disclaimer to non-equity partners reading this: The last thing I'm saying is that you don't contribute value, and the last thing I'm saying is that you don't work hard. All I'm saying is that among your counterparts in the non-equity partner law firm productivity food chain, you work fewer hours and cost the firm, and presumably clients, more.)

But we're talking about excess capacity.

Firms in an industry with excess capacity face an almost irresistible compulsion to cut prices, even to unprofitable levels. The goal is simply to keep people busy, in service of keeping the firm alive and satisfying clients, and in the hope that once market conditions recover, everything can get back to normal.

A hyper-rational manager might argue that cutting costs to the level that matches revenue is the only path that makes sense, and (rationally) that's correct, even inarguable. But that's hard, because the vast bulk of the costs in a law firm are people, starting with lawyers and starting among lawyers with partners and the most expensive non-partners.

And because it's hard, by and large that's not what we've done. Nor, I might add, are we remotely at risk of aping hyper-rational managers.

So we are faced with excess capacity. Which leads to intense pricing pressure. Which leads to lower profits. Which leads to: I leave it to your imagination.

3: EXPECTATIONS

Our third chapter addresses partner expectations. Here's the problem: There's about to be a collision with reality.

Let's start with some data. In the quarter century since the THE AMERICAN LAWYER first published the AmLaw 100, growth has been impressive:

- Total gross revenue for the 100 firms has gone up more than tenfold, from $7-billion to $71-billion, a Compound Annual Growth Rate of 9.71%.
- Average PPP has more than quadrupled, from $324,500 to about $1.4 million, 6.02% CAGR.
- And the average AmLaw 100 partner's earnings have gone from 11.3 times the average American employee's compensation to 23.4 times that benchmark in 2010 (the last year for which data is available).

Yes, the first two figures, for revenue and PPP, are in nominal (non-inflation-adjusted) terms, but the third most assuredly is not. With exceptions hardly worth mentioning, over the past two decades PPP in the AmLaw 100 has outpaced inflation (graphic courtesy Jomati Consultants):

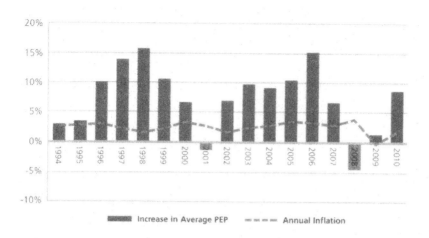

Table 2: Average PEP growth vs US inflation, AmLaw 100 law firms.

This is not just a statistically impressive run of the first order: It has real human implications.

Simply put, many (most?) of your partners have never experienced a seriously down year - OR EVEN A YEAR WHEN THEIR COMPENSATION GROWTH DIDN'T TROUNCE THE INFLATION RATE. It gets worse. These are averages, of course, which don't reflect the trajectory of any of the thousands and thousands of individual partners. I recently met with the managing partner of an AmLaw 10 firm who had done the analysis, and he said that the vast majority of people who were partners in 2007, before the Great Reset, and were still partners, had done very nicely indeed, simply by virtue of moving up the compensation ladder.

Other industry observers (not managing partners—they're far too diplomatic to say this, even if they might be thinking it) have told me in private that there are far too many people earning way more than they're worth; their success owes to being in the right place at the right time. Now, before the protests start coming in: (a) yes, they have worked really hard for many years to get where they are and stay there; (b) without exception, they're very smart and articulate; and with rare exceptions, they're also astute; and (c) it's a highly competitive market.

But going from 11.3X average nationwide compensation to more than double that? Name another industry where that's occurred to tens of thousands of people.

Investment banking? Guess again: Attrition is spectacular, as are bare-bones lean years even if you survive more than half a dozen years.

Medicine? While figures are hard to come by, Yale Medical School reports that the median physician's income in 1998 was 4.8 times that of the median full-time worker. Today, the median HOUSEHOLD INCOME in the US is just over $50,000 (US Census Bureau) while the average physician income is about $155,000, so the multiple is probably less than 4.8 today. I grant you that the conceptually correct comparison is between the "median physician" and the "median law firm partner," and then between the "AmMed 100" physician and the AmLaw 100 partner, but since the AmMed 100 doesn't exist, use your imagination. Do you really think there are thirty to forty thousand doctors earning nearly 25 times median US personal income?

By contrast, what do AmLaw 100 partners expect? More of the same; why wouldn't they? It's unlikely they'll admit this, of course: It's uncouth to complain that earning $1.4-million/year isn't enough. Except they think it, because:

- They compare themselves to corporate CEOs, the aforesaid i-bankers, and of course partners at That Other Firm whose PPP is 115% of ours;

- Like Parkinson's Law of work (which expands to fill the time available), household expectations, a/k/a "lifestyle," grow to absorb the income available. Have you heard, "I owe it to my family to take what the market is offering"? I have; it's unbecoming. You have no obligation whatsoever to have a luxurious second home (or a second home at all), multiple new BMWs or Audis, annual vacations all over the globe, and the list goes on.

- Did I mention that they've never experienced more than the odd year, by happenstance, when their compensation didn't handily outpace inflation?

There's a deeper problem, and it goes to the heart of what it means to be a one-firm firm, or a Partnership in the first place.

It better not be all about the money.

This has two sides to it: First, why partners are too often tempted to leave for a bump in income, and second, the challenges managing partners face in keeping firms pulling together in straitened times.

I have long believed that if someone leaves for (say) a 15% raise, they'll leave again for another 15%. They don't, in short, see themselves as a partner, but as captain of their own ship, master of their own destiny. I don't use these grandiose phrases lightly; people can too readily succumb to the temptation to think they've accomplished everything on their own.

I have news for you: The platform you're on, be it an AmLaw 10 or an NLJ 350, has far more to do with your success than you care to admit. You may think you're scoring all the goals, but you belong to a team. Try hanging out your own shingle and see how long your bountiful paydays last.

And from the management side: Keeping all the oars pulling together is enough of a challenge in the best of times. Explaining why ever-rising expectations cannot realistically be met without melting down the firm (cf. Howrey, Dewey) is doubly hard.

Add to that, that most lawyers don't understand business, including their own firm's business, and aren't honestly curious about it. Yes, they'll politely pretend they are, but 95% aren't really. This makes the managing partner's challenge of explaining why this tree has stopped growing to the sky almost insurmountable.

In short, you have implacable economic reality on one side and deeply ingrained learning, strongly reinforced by a bedrock belief that precedent is the surest guide, on the other. This is not a recipe for stability.

******

In September 2012 the recruiting firm Major, Lindsey and Africa announced, "Report Shows Pay Gaps Widening Among Partners", which outlined the results of a survey that drew 2,228 responses from partners at AmLaw 200, NLJ 350, and AmLaw Global 100 firms. The headline findings are:

- Equity partners, a/k/a rainmakers (relatively speaking, at least) make more than non-equity partners. (We really needed a survey to tell us this?)

- Men make more than women - to the shocking tune of 47% more ($734,000 vs. $497,000). What decade are we in, people? If this isn't reprehensible on its face, please explain in 25 words or less why not.

- And partners in firms with open compensation systems earn 74% more than those in closed systems ($810,000 vs. $465,000). I find this odd in the extreme, and have no handy-dandy explanation for it. Major Lindsey offers up that it's due to different response rates, with open-system partners "reporting significantly larger books of business than their closed system peers," but I don't think that gets you to a 74% delta. Any ideas here?

Lest you doubt my assertion in the original chapter that partners harbor the belief that "earning $1.4-million/year isn't enough," the article concludes thus:

Partners of all classes and genders were united on one front: They all think they should be making more money. Fifty-eight percent of all partners said they should be better paid, and among that group, an overwhelming majority wants something more than a token raise. Ninety percent of the survey's respondents thought that their compensation should be increased by more than 10 percent, while 1 percent thought their pay should be doubled.

Q.E.D.

4: ECONOMIES I & II

For some time, I've been struggling with how to characterize in pithy short-hand what our industry has been experiencing since almost four years ago to the day when Lehman Bros. collapsed.

How about Economy I and Economy II?

I steal the phrase from the iconoclastically wide-ranging David Brooks of *The New York Times* who in late 2012 wrote a column ostensibly about the Chicago school system's teachers' strike, but it was actually immensely broader than that.

Here's how he began:

Modern nations have two economies, which exist side by side. Economy I is the tradable sector. This includes companies that make goods like planes, steel and pharmaceuticals. These companies face intense global competition and are compelled to constantly innovate and streamline. They've spent the last few decades figuring out ways to make more products with fewer workers.

Economy II is made up of organizations that do not face such intense global competition. They often fall into government-dominated sectors like health care, education, prisons and homeland security. People in this economy believe in innovation, but they don't have the sword of Damocles hanging over them so they don't pursue unpleasant streamlining as rigorously. As a result, Economy II institutions tend to get bloated and inefficient as time goes by.

As I was reflecting on what Brooks had to say, I wondered if BigLaw has existed in Economy II essentially for...well, forever. But now it's being dragged into Economy I.

Understand what I am, and am not, proposing.

Does BigLaw face "intense global competition?" *Absolutely*, but until now it's been within and among other BigLaw members.

Is it government-dominated? Not remotely.

Does it have the sword of Damocles hanging over it? I have argued it does, but persuading a room full of people earning $1.4-million/year (average AmLaw 100 PPP last year) to that view can be awkward.

Is what BigLaw provides really tradable, in the same sense as planes, steel, and pharmaceuticals? Not yet, and some of will never be.

Do we face a compulsion to constantly innovate and streamline? You be the judge. If we do, there is scarcely a scintilla of evidence that anyone is making the smallest move in that direction.

So what am I talking about?

My thesis is that until now, the BigLaw stool has rested one leg in Economy I and two legs in Economy II, but that irresistible forces—the same forces that have proven their mettle by forcing revolutions in agriculture a century ago, followed by manufacturing (apparel, automobiles, machinery, furniture and appliances, consumer goods, electronics, etc.), followed by non-face-to-face services (call centers, finance and accounting, tax preparation, software coding, etc.)—are finally assaulting BigLaw.

If you must label these forces, they come into play where globalization meets technology, and there's an odd thing about both globalization and technology: Whether or not to embrace them *is not a choice.* In other words, the combined impact of these forces is pushing all three legs of the BigLaw stool into Economy I—like it or not.

******

Interlude and point of order:

This book talks about BigLaw, or SophisticatedLaw, as an industry. I'm not talking about individual firms or even segments of the market or groups of firms.

Will some firms continue to experience growth (as several private commenters have protested)? *Of course.* If my thesis is right, does that imply other firms will experience the euphemistically named phenomenon "negative growth"? To an arithmetic certitude, yes.

And here, as I talk about BigLaw moving into Economy I, I speak in the context of this series. I'm talking about the industry, not Marty Lipton, Ted Wells, or David Boies—or the fortunate firms they belong to. To ask whether they are threatened by the ascendancy of Economy I is akin to asking whether Ferrari noticed the Japanese auto invasion of the US.

******

Back to the Economy I/Economy II discussion. You may think we've been under serious client pressure on fees since, say, September 2008, and I readily concur. And you might think that means we're dealing with Economy I pressures. As I see it, not even close.

The history of responding to pricing pressure in BigLaw through "innovation" has been almost exclusively the story of labor market arbitrage. We have never gotten serious about changing the way we work.

By "labor market arbitrage," I mean finding (a) cheaper people; (b) cheaper locales; (c) cheaper career paths; (d) cheaper offices, or some combination of all of these, to be able to deliver a service of indistinguishable quality for less. This works, and for a while it gives clients what they want. But it has a few intrinsic limitations:

- These savings are one-off's. You can only move certain people out of midtown Manhattan once, and you can only introduce the non-partner associate track once.
- There are virtually no barriers to entry in the labor market arbitrage business. If AmLaw firm A can do it, so can AmLaw firm B, C, D,...—not to mention the Pangea3's and Integreon's of the world.

- Finally, "arbitrage" only succeeds as a profitable strategy, in equity and fixed income markets and in lawyer labor markets, so long as *there are inexplicable price differentials*. Once those "inexplicable" price differentials have been ironed out of the system and all that remain are fair, supply/demand driven, price differentials (based on quality, responsiveness, consistency, reputation, or other variables clients will pay for), there is no further profit to be made.

I challenge you to name one so-called innovation in our industry, introduced in the name of cost-cutting and efficiency, that has not at root been an exercise in labor market arbitrage.

We have not fundamentally changed how we do things. We have changed who does them and where. Economy II permits us to stop there; Economy I will require us to go much farther.

But like Bartleby, we prefer not to.

While every other sophisticated professional services industry uses behavioral interviewing and personality profiling to evaluate candidates, we prefer not to.

While business process re-engineering has come to virtually every company of scale in every industry, and all its divisions, we prefer not to.

While other industries are driven to do their utmost to excel at client service, we (let's be honest) pay it lip service on the surface and disdain it where it matters most, in terms of transparent value for transparent money.

And did I mention?

While other industries have relentlessly upended, rein-vented, re-engineered, six-sigma'ed, and kaizen'd themselves, while being under the constant unforgiving glare of creative destruction, we are using fundamentally the same business model Paul Cravath invented over a century ago. Change? We prefer not to.

Why?

Because we're lawyers. We know better. We know better than all of them.

5: INNOVATION

Now well on our way into *Growth is Dead*, it's only fair to offer up what we hope are some constructive ideas on how to deal with this phenomenon going forward.

But first, a quick recap of some of the things we've touched upon:

- From more or less 1980 until approximately September 15, 2008, the industry of BigLaw enjoyed an unprecedented run of growth in revenue, profitability, and headcount, with compound annual growth rates in the middle to high single digits for virtually that entire period, with only the occasional hiccup.
- This is almost unheard of in modern economies, and the Rothschilds could tell you a thing or two about the impact of that level of CAGR for that period of time (hint: it's how they made their fortune).
- The only other industries I can think of that rival anything like that kind of track record are nascent ones - say automobiles at the turn of the last century. (We're not a nascent industry.)
- Everything changed with the Great Reset.
- Clients, who had always had power but might not have known or exercised it, realized they did and they could. This will not change back.
- Pricing pressure is here to stay.
- The traditional bimodal career path within law firms, associate and partner, has multiplied into a large, and growing, variety of ways to work for BigLaw:
  - partner-track associates

- non-partner-track associates
  - staff, temporary, and contract lawyers
  - flex-time, work-at-home, and sabbatical-leave tracks
  - "of counsel" and non-equity partner positions
  - partners or former partners now serving full-time in management roles
- The BigLaw industry suffers from excess capacity on several levels, including
  - a surfeit of JD graduates being churned out by US law schools
  - too-high levels of leverage among traditional associate ranks
  - overpopulated ranks of non-equity partners
  - underperforming equity partners
- And excess capacity at the most fundamental level, I fear, means too many undifferentiated firms chasing too much of the same types of business, and tempted to engage in short-sighted, self-defeating pricing to keep revenue flowing.

Enough diagnosis. How about some prescription?

If you could take one and only one concept away from this series, it's this:

(1) Other industries, including professional service industries, have been dealing with all these challenges and more for a long time.

(2) We could learn a few things from them.

As Exhibit A I've chosen Procter & Gamble under the leadership of its CEO A. G. Lafley.

What does P&G sell? Products such as Crest, Tide, and Pampers. What's their intrinsic growth rate? Same as population growth. Not only that, but by the time of Lafley's ascension, P&G had become a $70-billion/year enterprise. Even 4-6% annual growth would require building a brand-new $4-billion/year business every single year. What could you possibly do to accomplish this?

Lafley bet on innovation. Pause to understand how the market landscape confronting Lafley at P&G in 2000 resembled the landscape that I believe is confronting BigLaw today:

- P&G's "intrinsic" growth rate more or less tracked population growth;
- Our "intrinsic" growth rate more or less tracks global GDP growth, with perhaps a slight bonus for increasing cross-border transaction volume and the steady march of regulation's complexity quotient.

Back to Lafley and innovation.

This from a 2006 *Harvard Business Review* case study, "P&G's New Innovation Model." Here's the introduction:

Editor's note: Procter & Gamble has operated one of the greatest research and development operations in corporate history. But as the company grew to a $70 billion enterprise, the global innovation model it devised in the 1980s was not up to the task. CEO A. G. Lafley decided to broaden the horizon by looking at external sources for innovation. P&G's new strategy, connect and develop, uses technology and networks to seek out new ideas for future products. "Connect and develop will become the dominant innovation model in the twenty-first century," according to the authors, both P&G executives. "For most companies, the alternative invent-it-ourselves model is a sure path to diminishing returns."

And here's what Lafley had to say about where innovation is occurring in today's economy. Not in the big institutions:

We discovered that important innovation was increasingly being done at small and midsize entrepreneurial companies [including] access to talent markets throughout the world. And a few forward-looking companies like IBM and Eli Lilly were beginning to experiment with the new concept of open innovation, leveraging one another's (even competitors') innovation assets — products, intellectual property, and people.

As was the case for P&G in 2000, R&D productivity at most mature, innovation-based companies today is flat while innovation costs are climbing faster than top-line growth.

We knew that most of P&G's best innovations had come from connecting ideas across internal businesses. And after studying the performance of a small number of products we'd acquired beyond our own labs, we knew that external connections could produce highly profitable innovations, too. Betting that these connections were the key to future growth, Lafley made it our goal to acquire 50 percent of our innovations outside the company. The strategy wasn't to replace the capabilities of our 7,500 researchers and support staff, but to better leverage them. Half of our new products, Lafley said, would come from our own labs, and half would come through them.

It was, and still is, a radical idea. As we studied outside sources of innovation, we estimated that for every P&G researcher there were 200 scientists or engineers elsewhere in the world who were just as good — a total of perhaps 1.5 million people whose talents we could potentially use. But tapping into the creative thinking of inventors and others on the outside would require massive operational changes. We needed to move the company's attitude from resistance to innovations "not invented here" to enthusiasm for those "proudly found elsewhere." And we needed to change how we defined, and perceived, our R&D organization — from 7,500 people inside to 7,500 plus 1.5 million outside, with a permeable boundary between them.

The proof was in the pudding, and the model worked: From 2000 to 2006, the proportion of new products on the market that included one or more elements originating outside P&G went from 15% to 35%, an increase of 133%, and the number of P&G brands generating a billion dollars or more in annual revenue was up to 22.

Essentially, what Lafley led P&G to do was to introduce completely new ways of doing old things (Swiffer) or slightly different ways of doing old things that consumers perceive as better, hence more valuable (how many iterations of Crest are on the market now compared to a dozen years ago?).

In other words, faced with the implacable obstacle of the rate of population growth as a presumed ceiling on P&G's growth rate, Lafley routed around it and chose to answer a question not posed by the premise.

I challenge you to name a single law firm thinking in that fashion. And I pose the immediate follow-up: Why not? Finally, one last challenge in the form of a few lessons, from Lafley: In May 2008 he was interviewed at Harvard Business School and the moderator summarized his takeaway as follows. I've added my thoughts in brackets following each:

1. In an age of disruption, growth is getting increasingly difficult. [That's precisely the point.]

2. Companies need to take the long view. Lafley said he finds it hard to watch CNBC for more than 7 minutes because the focus is so short term. [Thank goodness we don't have CNBC; may I point out we have now had PPP figures published for 25 years.]

3. The customer needs to be the center of the innovation equation. When Lafley took over as CEO in 2000, he said he saw too many managers on their cellphones, or buried in spreadsheets, in essence "showing customers their behind." [Ring a bell? Anyone?]

4. Experimentation is key. Lafley talked about the value of giving customers even crude prototypes to test an idea. He also described how different parts of his organization approach innovation differently, and that's a good thing. [Not directly applicable to us, perhaps, but when was the last time your firm showed a client a "crude prototype" of something you were thinking of doing? Thought not.]

5. Complex organizations need to simplify to successfully innovate. Lafley said he seeks Sesame Street simplicity. [When was the last time involving dozens of lawyers reduced complexity?]

6. The CEO has to be the "Chief External Officer" to manage external pressure and the "Chief Innovation Officer" to push the innovation agenda forward. [Neither of which roles comes naturally to most lawyers.]

To repeat, I dwelt on P&G under Lafley because they faced a market landscape with intrinsically limited growth, as do we, and he approached it in ways we would never dream of, including inviting ideas from outside the firm and developing totally new products in segments thought to be stagnant.

In late 2012 *The American Lawyer* published "The 2012 Global 100: A World of Change," which opens as follows:

The legal sector used to be such a nice, calm place to do business. Partners and clients would occasionally come and go. The odd practice would falter, while a few firms made slightly more money than everyone else. But the market historically lived up to its reputation as a bastion of sleepy conservatism and resilience. Then came the financial crisis, which forced the legal elite to adapt to the most turbulent market conditions for a generation.

As firms tussle for position in this new world order, the pronounced uptick in law firm merger activity has transformed our Global 100 rankings. New giants are emerging to dominate our charts, thanks in part to the increasing use of looser organizational structures that have facilitated these combinations.

The net result of all this change is that The Global 100 has become more top-heavy. The upper echelons of the international legal market, as measured by revenue, are becoming increasingly dominated by a smaller number of larger firms. And the gap is widening.

LegalWeek reported around the same time that the UK's top 20 law firms saw 439 partners leave in 2011 − 2012, "as firms continue to actively manage their partnerships." In particular, the Magic Circle posted partner departure rates of 2 − 4%, partly reflecting the "increased mobility of partners," but also "the trend for de-equitisations." Lest you think this is a post-Great Recession fad, here's what a leader of one, willing to be quoted on the record, had to say (emphasis mine):

A&O managing partner Wim Dejonghe said: "**Greater financial and operational discipline is definitely necessary in order to remain competitive in a low-growth environment.**

"For us, it's been a question of balancing the need for growth in the global network with continued focus on good housekeeping.

"The same challenges exist for all our competitors and everyone has to make a choice about where that balance lies and what's right for their business – **it's just a reality of the market we live in today.**"

On this side of the pond (although all these firms are global in the most profound sense), K&L Gates Chairman and CEO Peter Kalis was interviewed on the occasion of being re-elected to another five year term, and among other things had this to say (emphasis mine):

Kalis says his hardest day-to-day challenge is constructing a "modern business enterprise suitable for the 21st century." He likens the process of growing the K&L Gates brand, cultivating cutting-edge information technology, and managing the myriad other aspects of the firm's finances to "**building a bridge in wartime.**"

Both Dejonghe and Kalis, at the top of two of the largest law firms in the world, are telling us we're subject to the discipline of the market "in a low-growth environment," and that we must be 21st-Century business enterprises or...perish. I dwelt on A.J. Lafley and P&G earlier because they confronted these Darwinian pressures of the marketplace a dozen years ago, and responded in an enormously creative, not to mention successful, fashion. Will we have the imagination, the *applied* intellectual horsepower, and most critically of all the unswerving resolve, to do the same?

I wish I could tell you I have confidence in us all to do that.

I don't, and in the next chapter I'll try to explain why.

6: FAILURE

At the end of the last chapter, I opined that our industry needed to respond in creative and imaginative ways to the new market landscape, and that it would take "unswerving resolve" to do so effectively and successfully.

But I also warned that I don't have confidence in our ability to do that and promised to address why that's so in this chapter.

Also in the last chapter I spent some time discussing A. O. Lafley's tenure as CEO of Procter & Gamble, and that was no coincidence. To be sure, I applauded Lafley's embrace of innovation in an industry assumed to be mature and technologically placid—consumer packaged goods—but the fundamental reason I dwelt on P&G was that they compete in bruising consumer products categories where it's almost impossible to eke out growth above that of the population. (This is also true of Colgate-Palmolive, Kraft, General Foods and General Mills, Anheuser-Busch, etc., etc.)

All these firms—which are as sophisticated and re-sourceful as they come in marketing—are in a ceaseless battle for market share. If you talk to people in the trenches at these firms and their marketing and advertising agencies (I have), you know that they track market share with the intensity of a day trader watching the price of an options position. If that's a slight exaggeration, it is no exaggeration to say that market share matters as much as revenue or profits. And the reason is simple: To generate growth well above population trend, all these firms need to take market share away from their com-petitors. If Pampers (P&G) are to win, Huggies (Kimberly-Clark) must lose; it's a zero-sum game.

Sound like heavy weather? Well, we had best get used to it.

More importantly, these firms have had decades to hone and fine-tune their strategy, and they have been im-mersed in market-share wrestling matches for decades and decades—the entire lives of most brand managers and prod-uct development specialists. They're as good at this as it gets.

We don't even think this way; we don't want to think this way; and we have little clue where to begin if think this way we must.

Our problem is we don't have decades to figure it out.

But that's not our only problem, or even our biggest problem.

Not to channel Shakespeare, but our biggest fault lies within ourselves. In order to succeed in this new environ-ment:

- We must fundamentally change the way we do things: we must, in other words, innovate;

- Innovation requires delving into the unknown;

- Exploring the unknown requires experimentation;

- Experimentation involves failure;

- And we cannot tolerate failure.

The last point—that we, being lawyers, cannot tolerate failure—is critical. All else is prelude.

Attend to exactly what I mean. I don't mean we would prefer not to fail; or that all else being equal success beats failure; or that too long a string of failures marks a loser.

No, I mean something far stronger: We are built to critique, to second-guess, to demand accountability and assign culpability. If the gas can or the tires on the Concorde or the securities offering blows up, someone is responsible and someone is going to pay. They should have known better (because we certainly do). It's their fault and they will be made to pay; justice will be done.

There's a further dimension.

Alone among the professions—I submit—we are statistically innumerate and implacable in our refusal to entertain probabilities, odds, reasoned judgments, and cost/benefit tradeoffs. Doctors know when heroic measures will be unavailing; engineers stress-test models of everything from bridges to airplane wings to calculate acceptable failure modes; architects can guess which roofs will blow off in Category 5 hurricanes; even dentists, for heaven's sake, know that fillings, caps, and crowns will eventually fail.

And entrepreneurs, of course, know that failure comes with the territory.

Much has been written about Silicon Valley's tolerance for, even celebration of, failure. Now that people have actually studied it, they've found it makes sense. Here's why, as explained a few months ago in INC.:

> "In the start-up world, **FAILURE** is almost synonymous with *learning experience*. Being a founder who has failed before signals to *the community that, one, you've done this before, and, two, you've gathered information on what doesn't work and are better armed to create something that does.*"

> *Daniel Isenberg, the founding executive director of the Babson Entrepreneurship Ecosystem Project, says to truly understand failure, it's necessary to look beyond the individual blip of a single start-up failing to gain wide user traction and going belly-up. It's also necessary to look past a given entrepreneur's track record.*

> *In Isenberg's eyes, it's a much broader picture. When geographies and their governments embrace start-up failures, they catalyze economic growth.*

"If you look at really entrepreneurial countries or regions, you see very high failure rates," he says. "Lots of businesses opening and closing. That churn is failure."

In other words, not punishing failure leads to stronger long-term growth.

Other industries, and companies, learn through failure. We bury our failures.

But this fault - and make no mistake, it's a categorical fault - is in our nature as lawyers.

We cannot willingly enter into situations where failure comes with the territory. We can't weather the criticism, can't risk the second-guessing, don't have the emotional fortitude or resilience to explain why what we did was a thoughtfully calculated risk and one we'd do again.

I submit that our rigid intolerance for failure is so extreme and ultimately perverse that it disables us from being capable of sound decision-making.

Going forward will require a different mindset.

Are we capable of it?

7: PSYCHOLOGY

At the end of the last chapter, I asked aloud whether we as lawyers are intellectually and emotionally capable of adapting to the new market landscape, suggested that adapting would require experimentation and—yes—failure, and noted that countries and industries that did not reflexively punish failure enjoyed stronger long-term growth.

Let's talk about that some more.

A key set of players facing us on the new landscape are lower-cost providers. They come in a variety of guises but all essentially embrace (you can say "exploit" if you prefer, not that it will help you in the least) clients' newly exercised power to demand more for less.

The founder and head of one of these firms, which is in the business of applying Six Sigma processes to document review, and which has demonstrated consistently and convincingly that their quality is immensely superior to that produced by BigLaw associates working on the same document sets, remarked fairly casually to me not long ago that "for every dollar of revenue we gain, BigLaw loses three." If you want to reduce what "disruption" means down to a size suitable for a T-shirt, this will do nicely.

But we're hardly the first industry to encounter lower-cost providers. How have other incumbents responded when such a threat arises? I'm sorry to report the track record is not all that reassuring.

In June 2010 McKinsey published WHEN COMPANIES UN-DERESTIMATE LOW-COST RIVALS which opens thus:

> When low-cost competitors appear, one of the toughest decisions facing executives in companies with premium products and brands is whether to respond. Should the company or business unit adjust its strategy to meet the low-cost threat or should it continue business as usual, with no change in strategy or tactics?

Often, the incumbents' slow response stems from the most rational, admirable, and correct of motives: They're focused on their core customers and clients, who are not patronizing the low-cost new entrants. But markets, competitors, and technology—not to mention clients' tastes and preferences—are never static. The newcomers want to move up the value chain as badly as anyone, and often they find they can do so:

> As these established companies attempt to define the nature and magnitude of the challenge, they often underestimate it. Sometimes executives are so focused on their traditional competitors, they don't even recognize the threat developing from low-cost rivals. What executive isn't familiar with the case of the low-cost airline Ryanair and its hugely successful entry into the European market at the expense of the region's traditional carriers? Likewise, were the world's leading telecommunications companies too busy competing with one another to recognize the threat from the Chinese low-cost competitor Huawei, now a leader in fixed-line networks, mobile-telecommunications networks, and Internet switches? Then there was Vizio, a little-known LCD TV supplier that overtook the premium brands in five years to become the North American market leader in large-format TVs. Complacency and arrogance pro-

duce blind spots that delay a response and leave incumbents vulnerable.

It can be a mistake to think one has a reliable pricing umbrella over one's head. Even though Xerox first commercialized and introduced copiers into the US market, to the point where "xerox" became a verb like "google" is today, they never saw the threat coming from Canon, which introduced low-cost, low-feature-set machines into the US and in short order owned all but the very top end of the market.

By contrast, when DuPont introduced nylon, it priced it not at what a patent-owning monopolist could persuade the market to bear, but at what DuPont anticipated its costs of production would be, together with a modest profit margin, five years hence after going through the learning curve. This alternative approach accomplished two things: Not only did it make it all but impossible for new entrants to match DuPont's economies of scale when the technology became generic, but it induced DuPont customers to discover completely unforeseen uses for nylon (such as, to use a wild example, in women's stockings during the WWII silk shortage), which greatly increased DuPont's nylon revenues and accelerated their advances in optimizing production efficiencies.

Low-cost entrants have upset apple carts in everything from California premium wines to IT services, software development, pharmaceuticals, flavors and fragrances, and retailing.

Even if the incumbents react adroitly and nimbly, as viewed with the benefit of hindsight, they are almost invariably plunged into a highly stressful period of experimentation, hastily arranging an array of responses, which require those who lived through the experience to try first this and then that: Experimenting, in other words.

Earlier in this series I discussed what A. O. Lafley achieved at Procter & Gamble, with innovation in a seemingly mature market, but I didn't tell you what he said about failure. Essentially, it was: (a) fail **fast**; and (b) don't fail the same way twice. Doing this gracefully and effectively requires a personality characteristic that the psychological and organizational dynamics literature usually refers to as "resilience."

Indeed, resilience is so important to particular companies that assessment tools have been developed specifically to measure for it in individuals. One of the originals, the Caliper Profile, was developed in 1964 to help a life insurance company select agents who were naturally effective salesmen. Now, few lines of work are ever going to involve as much rejection (call it "failure") as life insurance sales. But the Caliper Profile also scores people on 17 other personality traits, and by this point has been administered to over 4-million college graduates in the US, as well as to some 3,000 lawyers. (What follows is courtesy of work Dr. Larry Richard, one of the leading authorities on lawyer personality types, has done.)

On six of the 18 traits, lawyers in general score one or more standard deviations above or below the population norm. No other professional group produces a profile that is systematically such an outlier from the norm. Here are the six traits in question:

Trait	US Population Average	Lawyers Average
Skepticism	50th %-ile (by definition)	90th %-ile
Autonomy	50%	89%
Abstract Reasoning	50%	81%
Urgency	50%	71%
Resilience	50%	30%
Sociability	50%	7% (12% if you include rainmakers)

Let's clarify something right away: If you're in the market for a lawyer, these are probably just the traits you're looking for---or at least four of them are. Let's say a powerful government agency has opened a high-profile investigation into your company, and you need a law firm. Here's how these four traits can work to your advantage:

- **Skepticism**: Do you want an advocate who is tempted to take what the agency says at face value, or someone who will challenge them at every turn?

- **Autonomy**: Do you want an advocate who can figure out what to do on their own, without micro guidance?

- **Abstract reasoning**: Need I say more?

- **Urgency**: This means our overwhelming need to get things done **now**. Great, for clients.

The last two traits may not be so ideal:

- **Sociability**: This refers to how readily one initiates new, intimate, emotionally vulnerable connections with others and sharing intimate details. (It's thus different than "gregariousness" or "extraversion," which relate to one's comfort level with small talk and to situations such as parties full of strangers.) Low Sociability means some lawyers may struggle to build and sustain a relationship that would reinforce their representing you.

- **Resilience**: Ah, the critical factor in rebounding from being rejected. Think of it as an indicator of sturdiness in the face of setbacks or criticism, as well as the ability to bounce back speedily. You might think that's not an issue since your chosen lawyers haven't been rejected; they've been selected. So low resilience isn't germane, is it? Not so fast. Low resilience also makes one more likely to respond poorly to stresses caused by change, uncertainty, and challenges. So you actually want an advocate with high resilience (good luck finding one) because when an adversary, a judge, or you-the-client criticize their thinking, challenge the bill, or even reject them for other unrelated work, the more defensive, even unhinged, they may become.

Now switch hats. You're the managing partner of a firm staring down the throat of the need for fundamental change. How do these lawyerly traits work in this context?

- **Skepticism**: Ready to be challenged at every turn, over matters great and small? Then this is the team you want to lead. True story: The managing partner of an AmLaw 50 mentioned at a partners' lunch that they were going to change the font size of the firm's letterhead by 2 points. 90 minutes later they were still debating the font size change. I actually don't know whether the change went through or not. Now expand that to a decision that actually has consequences, and have fun.

- **Autonomy**: These are people who really do not want to be led.

- **Abstract reasoning**: You can find holes in anything. Lawyers will.

- **Urgency**: When you're talking about the changes that have to be made, lawyers will focus on everything that's wrong with it. (There's that high Skepticism again.) When they go back to work, they'll forget about it entirely because they'll be preoccupied with the issues of the moment. Not the best way to build long-term consensus. Or, if partners will talk about the firm's long-run strategy, they'll tell you they have 15 minutes to devote to it; then you can come back in five years when we see how it turned out.

- **Sociability**: A growing body of research including the 75-year-old longitudinal "Harvard Grant Study" (following male grads of guess where?) is reinforcing the view that "this factor is the single most important predictor of all things good in the life of human beings who thrive" (Dr. Larry Richard), including work, life, and marital satisfaction. Particularly in times of disruptive change and dramatic uncertainty, high "sociability" can inoculate one against negativity, depression, poor team and cooperative skills, and psychological brittleness — and actually build Resilience.

- **Resilience**: Did we mention experimentation entails failure? And failure requires resilience?

All in all, it seems one could substitute "lawyer" for "pessimist" in Winston Churchill's famous dictum, and it would make equal if not greater sense:

An optimist sees the opportunity in every difficulty, a pessimist the difficulty in every opportunity.

Before you think we are presenting a counsel of despair, I submit that Churchill's apothegm may hold the key to our salvation. Understand that we are scarcely defenseless in the face of new entrants; they may have resources, so do we; they may have talented people, so do we; they may have enthusiastic clients, so do we.

The problem is that for the first time in a long time (a century?), change is not something to be suspicious and skeptical of; it has become something we must welcome and indeed embrace.

Twenty years ago, Peter Drucker wrote of "the five deadly sins" of management, and what he had to say is timeless:

> Recent years have seen the downfall of one once-dominant business after another - General Motors, Sears Roebuck and IBM, to name just a few. In every case the main cause has been at least one of the five deadly business sins - avoidable mistakes that harm the mightiest business.

Here are those sins (mostly a paraphrase or verbatim quote of Drucker, emphasis mine):

- The first and easily the most common is the **worship of high profit margins and of 'premium pricing'.** This was Xerox's downfall in the face of Canon's entry into the copier business, and GM, Ford, and Chrysler's in the face of first the VW Beetle and later the Japanese. Drucker's lesson: the worship of premium pricing always creates a market for the competitor. And high profit margins do not equal maximum profits. Rather, maximum profit is obtained by the profit margin that yields the largest total profit flow, and that is usually the one that produces optimum market standing.

- Closely related to this first sin is mispricing a new product by **charging 'what the market will bear'**. This, too, creates risk-free opportunity for the competition.

- The third deadly sin is **cost-driven pricing**. Most American and practically all European companies arrive at their prices by adding up costs and putting a profit margin on top. And then, as soon as they have introduced the product, they have to cut the price, redesign it at enormous expense, take losses and often drop a perfectly good product because it is priced incorrectly. Their argument? 'We have to recover our costs and make a profit.' This is true, but irrelevant. **Customers do not see it as their job to ensure a profit** for manufacturers. The only sound way to price is to start out with what the market is willing to pay - and thus, it must be assumed, what the competition will charge - and design to that price specification.

- The fourth of the deadly business sins is **slaughtering tomorrow's opportunity on the allure of yesterday**. It is what derailed IBM. IBM's downfall was paradoxically caused by unique success - catching up, almost overnight, when Apple brought out the first personal computer in the mid- 1970s. But then, when IBM had gained leadership in the PC market, it subordinated this new and growing business to the old cash cow, the mainframe computer.

- The last of the deadly sins is **feeding problems and starving opportunities**. All one can get by 'problem-solving' is damage containment. Only opportunities produce results and growth. I suspect that Sears Roebuck has been starving the opportunities and feeding the problems in the retail business these past few years. The right thing to do has been demonstrated by GE, with its policy of getting rid of all businesses - even profitable ones - that do not offer long-range growth and the opportunity for the company to be number one or number two worldwide. Then it places its best-performing people in the opportunity business, and pushes and pushes.

Did you note what I noted about what all but one of these five have in common? Four of the five have to do with **price**.

And isn't "price" what has been driving us to distraction ever since the Great Reset? "Clients are demanding value." "Realization hits all-time lows." "Annual rate increases don't work the way they used to." "No junior associates on our matters." "Purchasing managers on review panels."

It's all about price.

The market is trying to tell us something. My counsel would be to listen. My thoughts on how exactly to go about that will be in the next chapter.

8: Now What?

If you've traveled this far, you may be wondering what I think you actually ought to *do*.

Recognizing that diagnosis is easier than prescription, the remaining chapters—starting with this one—will try to address that. One other caveat: Not all of what I'm going to suggest will be advisable, or even applicable, to all firms; this is where your judgment and knowledge of the particular historic path and current capabilities and limitations of your firm come into play. But if you'd like to talk about any of that, you know where to find me.

Mindset change #1: You do have competition

Countless are the times I've asked firms or individual partners who they perceive their competition to be, and the odds are about 9 in 10 that the response coming back is, "Well, no one, really."

False and double-false.

And no, I do not care how high up into the stratosphere of prestige you care to go, *you have competition.* (Even David Boies and Ted Olson have each other, after all.)

So stop pretending otherwise and begin to figure out what you're going to do about it.

Other firms are going after your existing clients all the time. And if you're not going after theirs, why not? Even in the good old days, there was no entitlement to incumbency — be it in a client relationship, an AmLaw ranking, or a recruiting bakeoff. In today's world of one great big battle for market share, there's almost negative entitlement to incumbency. If you're not fighting to expand your share, you're probably sliding backward.

The Econ 101 type of competition comes from other firms who are basically doing the same thing you do: Camrys and Accords, Corn Flakes and Wheaties, Benjamin Moore and Sherwin Williams, AT&T and Verizon, AmLaw XX and Am-Law YY. You fight these types of competitors largely on the dimensions of price/value, quality/expertise, and service/responsiveness. I hope you know how to win your fair share of work from what are essentially "me too" competitors. (If you don't, I need to be writing another book than this one.)

But you also need to understand something slightly more nuanced — and enormously more threatening — about competition. This is the concept of "substitutes." Substitutes are an indirect, subtler form of competition, because a substitute for your services is not exactly equivalent. It's something that, given the right tradeoff between price and quality, can be equivalent or better in the eyes of the client. Classic examples are tea and coffee, margarine and butter, or heating oil and natural gas.

You can watch this play out from home. During shortages caused by war, crop failures, or other abnormal circumstances, coffee drinkers may be driven to tea or tea drinkers to coffee. Some who switched may find they actually prefer the substitute. Similarly, if "fracking" ends up vastly increasing the recoverable reserves of natural gas in the United States, we can expect it to displace heating oil in many uses—some of which will be permanent changes. This is the reason substitutes can be more threatening in the long run than classic competitors: The client may come to prefer the substitute and never return to the original good/service even when circumstances revert to normal. The client is gone forever.

Among other potential substitutes for the expertise of AmLaw XX are technology, bulked up inhouse departments (composed of lawyers and others such as compliance and risk management professionals), legal process outsourcers, and "doing without." (Don't underestimate doing without as a viable choice; does every corporation have to sue every potential patent, trademark, or copyright infringer, for example?)

Mindset change #2: Treat your business like a business

Many law firms are now globe-spanning, billion-dollar a year enterprises. This presents a sophisticated management challenge. Heck, even a $10-million/year firm has a respectable client base that has come to rely on it, not to mention providing all or a substantial component of the support to dozens of families. Treat it as the complex and dynamic organization it is.

Floating around in the management literature (I've tried to find the source but can't) is a rule of thumb that the complexity of managing a professional service firm is something on the order of 5X that of a conventional company in (say), retail or wholesale trade, manufacturing or construction or transportation. If you believe that's at least directionally correct (I do), then your $10-million/year law firm presents challenges equivalent to (say) a $50-million/year retail chain, and running a $1-billion/year law firm requires as much sophistication and expertise as running a $5-billion/year general economy business. (For perspective, Xerox is about a $20-billion/year business, and Hollywood ticket revenue is just over $10-billion/year.)

We can debate (and I invite readers to do so among yourselves) whether the proper multiple is 5X, 3X, 7X, or some other number, but what matters is something I think we can all agree on: It's >1X.

Don't shortchange what this requires.

To begin with, take a sober second look at whether you as Managing Partner can maintain a serious, active practice caseload and manage the firm. Your primary job is now management, not practicing. In what other industry with similar-sized enterprises is management pitching in on the assembly line as well?

Specifically, it requires accomplished senior-level people running the business side. I'm referring to specifically to your "C-Suite:" The firm's COO, CFO, CIO, CMO, head of HR, and maybe more.

If you or your partners think of these executives as "non-lawyers," stop reading. Not only is that demeaning to them, it reveals a fallacious and unattractive sense of superiority. For reasons that escape me but appear to be effectively widespread, lawyers are inclined to assume they can do anyone else's job but no one else could possibly do what they do.

Stated that way, it sounds absurd, no? But admit it: The thought has crossed your mind. Exterminate it.

Because if you don't, it becomes a self-fulfilling prophecy. Your firm (say) thinks the IT function is being handled if the network stays up and you can find your documents again where you saved them, so hires the most inexpensive IT leader you can find who exhibits baseline competence. Don't then complain if a competitor firm turns out to have far more robust and fluid collaboration tools, which clients enjoy the benefits of and come to appreciate.

Too many staffers are lapsed lawyers with little in the way of credentials (the JD does not count) or expertise in their functional areas. Partners are reassured by staffers having JDs? Wrong question. The question must be what the individual brings to serve the business needs of the firm.

Historically, perhaps the saddest example—with dashed expectations and "I told you so's" flying in all directions—has been the marketing function. Not so very long ago, marketing (or "Business Development," as it was often revealingly labeled) was too frequently staffed by junior people innocently promoted into roles they had no training for and whose job functions, truth be told, were largely those of advanced PowerPoint jockeys and party planners.

And what happened? When partners called on "marketing," nothing remotely transformative or strategic could possibly occur. When marketing failed to move any visible needles, partners condemned the marketing function as ineffective, which justified cutting spending, ensuring the firm could only hire the more of the greenest and least capable junior people, launching another round of marketing disappointments, and you get the idea.

That this is changing is the good news; that it ever happened to begin with teaches a lesson we'd best not forget. Treat your business like a business.

Mindset change #3: Indistinguishable strategies are...indistinguishable

Have you ever played the "Guess Which Firm's Website!" game? I have, and I recommend you try it when you have nothing better to do; don't worry, you'll get the point of the game inside of five minutes.

The rules are simple: Pick three or four firms at random, visit their websites, and pretend you can't see the logo identifying the firm. Try to guess which firm it is.

Variation 1: since it's awkward for most of us to ignore what's plainly in front of our eyes (the logo), ask yourself what would have to change on the site if you were to swap in entirely different firm's logo and identity. I'm talking about messaging, positioning, and *true* differentiators, not "mere facts" such as lawyers' names and office locations. I've taken a small random sample to spare you the exercise. These are paraphrases of key claims from four different AmLaw 100 firms' sites:

- Our lawyers share a common culture, supporting our firm-wide commitment to add value, achieve excellence, and promote professional development, as well as diversity and inclusion, pro bono service and community support.

- We are a premier international law firm with a diversified business practice, more than XXX lawyers, and offices in A, B, C, D, [etc.]. We have over ZZ years of serving a broad range of client interests.

- We are a global law firm with approximately XXX lawyers in YY offices. We are privileged to serve clients across the entire spectrum....

- We are a full-service law firm distinguished by our highly collaborative, cost-effective approach...

Please do not waste time trying to figure out which firms these are or presume for a second that I'm picking on them: I'm not. They were literally the first four that came to mind.

Before you think I tar all firms with the same brush, you can find exceptions: Firms that say something distinctive. But you have to look hard, and far and wide. Here are two I particularly like:

Momentum. Movement. Forward motion.

That is what we do at Proskauer. It's the foundation of any successful business. [...]

It's not enough to do good legal work. There are many firms out there and to be fair, most are capable of closing a deal or winning a case. It's hardly surprising. We went to the same law schools, learned the same legal principles and passed the same exams.

So what do we bring to the table?

Our approach is not simply to "represent" our clients but to get into their heads.

"Get into their heads?" Fabulous. Or this (Paul Weiss):

Statement of Firm Principles

Judge Simon H. Rifkind, 1963

Our objectives are, by pooling our energies, talents and resources, to achieve the highest order of excellence in the practice of the art, the science and the profession of the law; through such practice to earn a living and to derive the stimulation and pleasure of worthwhile adventure; and in all things to govern ourselves as members of a free democratic society with responsibilities both to our profession and our country. [And there's more.]

Because these are so rare, they have the indelible ring of truth. Compared to the first four I cited?

Put yourself in a client or prospective client's shoes. How could you possibly form an opinion of the differences between these firms, not to mention which might actually best serve your needs?

I submit it's actually worse than that. I bet partners of most firms couldn't even identify their own firm based on un-identified excerpts from their websites.

"There's a difference between a website and a strategy," I hear you objecting? Of course there is.

But without a window into the strategic planning pro-cess of a large sample of AmLaw firms, websites should rep-resent a rough proxy for who they think they are, what makes them distinctive, and how they express their difference and position themselves. The most important point is that *strategy matters* more than ever before. If you haven't seen these charts before (courtesy of the annual report out of the Citi Private Bank Law Firm Group), they should deliver that message more strongly than anything else I could say:

Profitability Distribution of US Law Firms (2005-07) ($000)

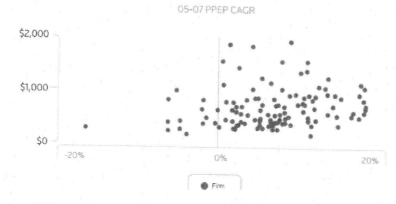

Source: Citi Private Bank Law Firm Group Long-Term Trend Analysis. Sample Size: 108.

A nice pretty concentration, no?

Now look at the post-Great Reset distribution:

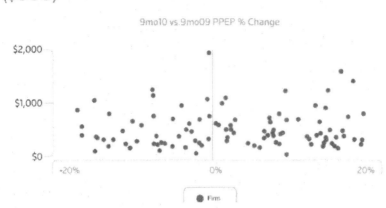

Profitability Distribution of US Law Firms (2010 Prelim.) ($000)

9mo10 vs.9mo09 PPEP % Change

Source: Citi Private Bank Law Firm Group Long-Term Trend Analysis, Sample Size: 106.

Our clean concentration has dissolved. In other words, strategy now matters.

A strategy that's a mishmash is no longer acceptable.

Loathe as you may be to admit it, I have news for you: If you can't articulate it plainly and crisply to the world, as on your website, it's a mishmash.

9: FUTURE MODELS

The first eight chapters, to state the obvious, have been all about the challenges facing BigLaw, which I believe may be mortal to some firms who don't or can't respond effectively. The new landscape reflects trends bubbling up under the surface for some time, including globalization and the relentless march of IT, spreading transparency into talent, ideas, and value for money, and all of which have been accelerated and brought into the clear light of day by the Great Reset of 2008 and beyond.

A rational reader might ask: "Is it all gloom and doom? Do you really think BigLaw will cease to exist as we know it?" Fair question, the answer to which is no.

In this chapter I want to describe what I believe the future of BigLaw, more or less "as we know it," may hold. I predict it will be:

- Smaller overall as an industry, in terms of revenue and headcount;
- Cylindrical rather than pyramidal at its organizational core;
- More cloud-like than either cylindrical or pyramidal in its reach;
- With an obsessive and intense firm by firm focus on delivering stringently defined services for carefully identified, and narrow, categories of clients.

You may have noticed I've said nothing there about profitability. That's because I believe the jury is out on that scorecard, but I see no intrinsic reason whatsoever that profitability need take a systemic plunge. Profitability will be far more dependent on smart and focused management than ever before; the days of "do no harm" and "steady as she goes" are gone forever, and room for error will be tightly circumscribed.

First let me lay out the reasons I believe BigLaw will continue to exist in some form we could agree is recognizable today, and then let me describe what adaptations creatures will have to make to survive and thrive in the new ecosystem. Think of the first part as demand and the second as supply.

Demand:

- Globalization is here to stay (see #3)
- Regulatory, precedential, and financial complexity is here to stay.
- The ability of talent, ideas, and capital to cross borders is here to stay (see #1)

Let's explore this a bit.

1. By "globalization" I'm really talking about the spread of multinational corporations. For example, the revenue GE derives from non-US operations crossed the 50% threshold a few years ago; it will never go back. For many industries, including some of the largest in the world, it would never cross anyone's mind to imagine they're *not* global by definition. Such as? How about oil and gas exploration, production, and refining; automobiles; aircraft and airlines; electronics; software; entertainment in all forms and media; sports; and the list goes on and on. It's almost simpler to talk about industries

that are constrained by laws of nature to remain local, which are increasingly limited to those where human beings have to interact in person to create and deliver the service: Restaurants, healthcare, residential construction, retailing.

The point is simply that the dynamics pushing whatever industries *can* go global *to* go global are unyielding, and there are no forces operating in the other direction.

2. By complexity I'm simply positing the commonplace observation that regulation, precedent, and financial tools are always being added to but never subtracted from. Dodd-Frank will never be repealed, nor will Sarbanes-Oxley before it, and if Glass Steagall was actually repealed it now stands a good chance of being replaced by the Volcker Rule, 1,000 pages and growing. The cumulative bulk of judicial decisions never shrinks, as more and more finely sliced distinctions can always be added (the US Supreme Court has discovered a difference under the Fourth Amendment's prohibition on unreasonable searches and seizures between homes and cars), and as scenarios never remotely contemplated by the drafters of constitutions, statutes, and regulations become reality: Does automatically captured GPS tracking data from your smartphone raise issues of "privacy?"

Similarly, financial derivatives (say) will never be "uninvented."

All of these complex systems exhibit ratchet-like behavior: Their interstices proliferate in only one direction, towards greater and greater complexity, since there are no intrinsically opposing forces, and there is no morbidity in their ranks.

3. Cross-border flows have never been at fuller tide, and speaking of tides the tide of history is running in favor of systematically eroding whatever legacy barriers (language, visa and immigration requirements) remain. Even China's economic boom cannot stop its most skilled professionals from seeking greater freedom abroad.

Nor is it an accident that the one practice area showing evidence of an increased pulse is intellectual property. Ideas are increasingly important to differentiate and distinguish goods and services when all generic characteristics can be replicated almost anywhere.

Similarly with capital flows: Not only have First World economies become continuously more open, but new capital "trade routes" are opening up between countries and regions where before there were none: Consider the emergence of the Brazil/China/Australia/Africa triangle, for example.

Need I point out that all these trends should bode well for BigLaw? Every single one alone, and all in combination, should create work for us.

But do, or how do, we need to configure ourselves to respond?

Supply:

Heretofore BigLaw has followed a remarkably homogeneous business model, with the result that even as knowledgeable and informed a follower of our industry as Aric Press has observed more than once that it's almost impossible to tell the difference among (say) AmLaw 25−75 firms.

This, I predict, will end.

It will end because clients will demand it, and they will vote with their dollars.

As they become increasingly sophisticated and discerning in how they select and purchase legal services, and as the CFO and yes, the purchasing department, increasingly look over the General Counsel's shoulder, I believe they will push our industry to evolve, at first barely perceptibly but in a rapidly accelerating fashion, towards a different fundamental composition, or ecosystem if you will.

These are species I predict will thrive, or falter, on this new landscape:

- The full-service, national or regional or super-regional, one-size-fits-all, not terribly specialized, generic law firm:
  - *Endangered and at risk of becoming marginalized.*
- Truly global players spanning three or more continents — and as many as six — who deploy a vast, but truly unified, network across virtually all economically meaningful jurisdictions.
  - *Top of the food chain predators eliminating less fit competitors*
- Boutiques exquisitely focused on doing one thing exceptionally well
  - *Survivors who know their niche in the ecosystem and stay close to it*
- "Category killer" specialists who target one broadly needed but perhaps not intrinsically high-value practice area
  - *Hungry and effective acquirers who will absorb anything on their turf and improve it*

Let's take these in reverse order.

Category killers have vanquished competition in many industries, most famously retail, where firms like Barnes & Noble, Home Depot, Toys 'R Us, Staples, and Best Buy have come to dominate their "categories." In some cases there's room for more than one firm per vertical niche (Home Depot has Lowe's, and Staples has Office Depot, but Best Buy finished off Circuit City), but regardless of the microstructure of the industry, the point is that one or more firms decided to focus on supplying one highly specific type of good/service and learned how to do it extremely well.

They don't do everything, but who cares? To the contrary, clients have exhibited a strong and lasting preference for firms that promise to do one thing very well and don't pretend to do anything else. There's a rationale behind their success:

- They don't get distracted;
- They can develop extraordinarily deep expertise;
- Customers can rely on the best selection of "X" being available;
- They can invest in systems, people, and processes specifically tailored to their vertical niche;
- And perhaps most importantly, these firms have staked out an extremely clear identity, so the "brand promise" to their customers is universally understood and strongly articulated.

Now, in Law Land, I would argue that we're beginning to see the emergence of some category killer firms as well: Think Jackson Lewis, Littler Mendelson, and Ogletree Deakins for employment, for example.

Also note: Once one or more firms begins to establish a powerful beachhead in category X, it becomes increasingly difficult, uneconomic, and unattractive, for other firms to offer X. They can't do it with as much expertise, or with as broad geographic coverage, or *for the price* of the category dominant firms. Note the last point: This may be the "secret sauce" to their success. I couldn't even hazard a guess how many times I've heard a law firm say, "we used to do employment law, but we just couldn't continue to do it for the rates the market demands."

Tough for other law firms, great for clients. QED.

One final parenthetical, just for thoroughness, before leaving this topic: There is, as yet, no equivalent in Law Land to the threat that online retailing poses to these brick and mortar firms. But all of them, Best Buy and Barnes & Noble perhaps most urgently, have to figure out a credible and durable response.

Boutiques have always been with us, and with almost any other industry I can think of. You might be tempted to think of them as close cousins of category killers, in that they do one thing and do it well, but they aren't really, since their model isn't necessarily premised on wringing cost out of service delivery through regularized and (to the extent possible) technology-enabled business processes and methods. Indeed, many boutiques have sky-high billing rates, just as Cartier, Ferrari, and Gulfstream (boutiques all, I would argue) position their offerings exclusively in the sky-high price tranche.

Moreover, the boutique model is far more flexible and extensible than the category killer model: There are only so many available categories, after all, that call for scale on the order of (say) Home Depot or Littler Mendelson, but boutiques are found everywhere.

Some species of boutiques are so familiar we may not even think of them as boutiques any more, but they are: The IP boutique or litigation boutique, for instance. In a totally separate market from BigLaw, we obviously have players concentrating on things like ~~divorce~~ family law, or plaintiff-side class action litigation.

Boutiques—as a business model, abstracting from the boutique's chosen subject matter—have several features to commend them:

- They know who they are, and their clients know who they are;
- They can avoid distracting and time-consuming debates about whether to launch new practices or cut back on existing ones;
- And the smallish size of the organization, and the commonalities among what everyone does within it, vastly simplify management.

The one systemic threat to boutiques arises from the roots of almost all of them in one or a handful of visionary founders or leaders. The risk is succession planning; there may not be any. But realize this isn't a flaw in the boutique model; it's a flaw in that particular endangered boutique's management.

If I'm right that we see boutiques throughout the economy, why is that? My best guess is that the fundamental reason boutiques are ubiquitous has to do with economies of scale, or rather the relative lack thereof in niches where boutiques thrive. A large part of the value of owning a Rolls Royce stems from its taking on the order of 400 man-hours to build, vs. 20 or less for a Toyota; a single person can spend an entire day selecting and matching sections of leather (all from the same animal's hide, mind you!). Toyota can't cope with that and isn't interested in trying.

This in turn stems from another deep fact about most markets: A certain small subset of customers in almost any market has a set of preferences so specialized, demanding, and dare I say "picky," that price almost ceases to matter. These are the multinational corporations or, more likely, individual moguls, who just have to have the latest G5 — or luxuriously customized 767, for that matter.

Where, in this taxonomy, you might be wondering, do the super-prestigious law firms fit? Cravath, S&C, Wachtell, Slaughter & May, Davis Polk, etc. — the New York and white shoe and London elite? Right here, folks: In the price is (almost) no object league.

Truly global powerhouses have a place in this ecosystem, first and foremost, because they have multinational corporate clients who need a matching footprint in their law firm. That's the primary reason many of these firms will survive, and thrive. (See "Demand," above.)

But there's a separate category of client that can benefit from capabilities these firms can provide that no one else really can, and they need not be globe-spanning enterprises in their own right at all: Indeed, they could be quite small. I have in mind clients who, because of the intrinsically global nature of the industry/market they're in, can benefit from a law firm ally with global reach. For example, imagine a small biotech or medical device manufacturer located in one of the US's local hotbeds of IP—maybe Research Triangle Park in North Carolina or Austin, Texas—who needs to connect with a manufacturing facility in a place like Taiwan or Vietnam. Wouldn't a globe-spanning law firm come in handy? And there aren't many "substitutes" (economic sense) for that kind of ally.

Note I have not discussed whether these globe-spanning law firms have to be at the "elite" end of the market, because I don't believe they do. There's room for high-end and middle-market players, and perhaps even some room for another level below that. How many? Well, pre-2008 everyone used to think there would be dozens and dozens. Not any more. My own money would be on the order of 15—20 firms, with:

- Flags planted at least in North America, Europe, and Asia
  - And maybe South America, Australia, and Africa
- Strong expertise in English and New York law
- And as much of a presence as regulatory authorities permit, in closed or quasi-closed but economically vital markets such as Brazil, Korea, and India.

Finally, **national or regional full-service**, but not particularly specialized, firms.

I fear that firms in this group are at risk of not being able to state a compelling value proposition to clients. If they can't, their competitive position will slowly erode and they could find themselves marginalized, certainly if doing any meaningful amount of high-end work is their aspiration.

Whereas the first three types of firms have, I believe, a credible and distinctive positioning that clients "get," and can deliver a tailored set of services difficult to duplicate through other structural forms of organization, firms in this group need to focus more rigorously than ever on precisely what it is that their particular firm offers to clients—and why clients should engage them to deliver it and not someone else. (Hint: It's not "superb lawyering.")

Firms in this category won't be able to find a "one size fits all" solution to their challenges. (Trust me, if I had such a solution I'd be pounding the pavement with it.) Rather, each firm will need to engage in an intensive, and challenging, process of articulating what they can do for clients that other firms can't, and communicate that to clients.

These firms may have to wrestle with what could be make-or-break decisions and initiatives about client management and client service.

What that means, and how to do so, will be the subject of our next chapter.

10: CLIENTS

In Chapter 8, we talked about "Now What?" in terms of three particular approaches you could take that were all, essentially, inward-focused and things you can pretty much control inside the firm's four walls:

- acknowledge you have competition;

- hire the best professional "C-suite" staff you can find; and

- articulate a non-generic strategy — and begin to execute it.

In this chapter I'd like to address the external landscape, and specifically its single most critical feature: Clients.

The legendary Peter Drucker used to enjoy stumping MBA students by asking, "What is the *one thing* every firm has to have?"

Answers typically ranged from "a product" to "cash" to "an idea" to "employees," but none of these is what Drucker was looking for. The one thing is: Clients.

Sometimes I have to wonder if we've gotten the message.

In thinking about the evolution of client service, these are the phases I see.

Phase I: Sell what you make

Firms in Phase I find a comfort zone of things they (as proud and unbending autonomous individuals) enjoy doing, and they assume without, I imagine, really giving it much conscious thought, that since they enjoy it clients will appreciate it, or because they find it interesting clients will too. This approach is neither introspective nor strategic, but it has, as mentioned, the advantage of being comfortable. You could think of the firm's pitch to a client amounting to this:

"I love trying cases; got a case I could try?"

Simplistic? No, I would argue it's merely distilling the approach down to its essence.

I'm not implying firms approaching things this way can't find clients, or satisfy them, but I do believe it's pretty much serendipitous when that happens. The lawyer may wake up every day hoping to try a case; I assure you no client wakes up with that lawyer in mind just on the off chance they get sued and suddenly need courtroom representation.

It does violence to the word "haphazard" to even describe this as a haphazard approach to business development; it's a fundamentally self-indulgent attitude towards the world, which is no approach at all. Here, the lawyer is the Sun at the center of the solar system around which all else revolves.

Phase II: Make what sells

Phase II is a bit more mature and purposeful. In this phase, lawyers and firms try to analyze what services clients are seeking and purchasing, and then attempt to mold their offerings to client demand. No cases for us to try? Well, if you're looking for a little alternative dispute resolution instead, we can do that for you. The distilled pitch is something like this:

"Just tell us what legal services you need, and we'll get right on it."

While this takes the lawyer out of the very center of the picture, and gives the client a bit of breathing room alongside, it's still passive and reactive. To begin with, what if the client doesn't know or can't articulate what they need? Worse, what if your firm really *isn't ideal* for what the client wants? In that case "making it" for them might not be doing them any favors.

It also short-circuits pretty much any thoughtful professional development or strategically guided growth of your firm, if you're constantly emulating a pinball responding to the latest entreaty from a client.

Phase III: Solve the client's problem

This phase has several characteristics to commend it:

- It goes straight to the heart of what the client needs professional counsel for;

- It's agnostic as to exactly which practice area or practitioner, if any, is best suited to the matter at hand;

- And most important by far, it postures the entire offering and engagement around what the client needs, not what you can do.

The distillation of this pitch might be:

"We wonder if XYZ is troubling you; we have some thoughts on that."

Note what is *not* said here: It's not about what the lawyers prefer to do or are in the mood to work on; nor how brilliant, experienced, and highly credentialed they are (though I'm confident they are exceptionally so); nor about how much other clients adore them and sing their praises; nor, finally, is it about the law firm at all. It's entirely about making the clients life easier, less worrisome, and letting them focus on their business and not this potential legal landmine.

A very wise managing partner, who had studied at the feet of one of the builders of a great New York law firm, once told me that his primary job was making the client look good: "The wins are theirs; the losses are mine."

If I haven't been clear, I believe very few firms indeed have achieved Phase III, emulated my friend, or even grasped the reality that with stagnant/declining demand for legal services from traditional law firms, and excess capacity in our sector, we're now in a battle for market share. In this environment, we have to treat our existing clients like gold because acquiring new clients means stealing them from some other firm where (one can only assume) they've been perfectly content heretofore.

Altogether too many of us lack any focus on what the implications of this are. I never want you just to take my word for it, so consider these findings from an ALM Survey released in late 2012:

- We're not serious about measuring client or partner profitability: Just 44% of those questioned said they were hitting their profit targets with individual clients and 46% with individual partners. These are flunking grades.

- We're not serious about requiring new measures of productivity and client pricing arrangements. Respondents' "top three" financial measurements included nothing but old school data: Firm revenue (52%), firm profit (44%), PPP (37%), utilization (30%), and operating margins (24%). Where is client satisfaction?

- Actually, ALM also told us how much we care about client satisfaction: A bare majority of firms even deign to track it. Although we all may declare with self-satisfaction that client service is crucial to our competitive advantage, only 56% reported that their firm has a plan in place to measure, track, and build client satisfaction and loyalty.

- And get this, which I found the most shocking finding of all: Four out of five respondents (78%) could not honestly say that their firm leaders were "extremely knowledgeable" about their top 20 clients' businesses.

I find the last point tantamount to client management misfeasance. Yet consider whether the reality might be even worse than our law firm respondents reported; they might just have an optimistic bias. Here's an example, from an *Inside Counsel* survey, of two quite distinct report cards on the "overall service level" of law firms:

Grade	In-house counsel	Law firm
A	19%	62%
B	70%	35%
C	10%	3%
D/F	0.5%	—

Or this: "Outside counsel always or usually understand the business issues." Agree:

- Clients: 22%

- Law firm partners: 92%

While we're at it, here's a roster of "value added" offerings from law firms to clients, and how clients rank the importance of the offerings vs. how law firms perform on them. In a nutshell, we do poorly on the important and we do just fine on the unimportant.

Offerings where clients grade importance more highly than law firms' performance (all listed in order of importance):

- Secondments

- Seminars at the client's office

- Regular service review meetings

- Seminars at the law firm's office

And offerings where clients grade the law firms' performance more highly than importance:

- One on one lunches

- Newsletters

- Pitching proactively for new work

- Websites

- Corporate hospitality

- Seeing a firm's name in the press

See a pattern emerging?

We have another problem with client management in a market-share-battle environment, and this problem stems from our own culture and psychology. Namely, it's more glorious to win a new client than it is to patiently nurture and grow the relationship with an existing client. Yet the data is utterly consistent that existing clients are more profitable than new clients, and that a stable roster of clients can lead to greater continuity internally in the firm in terms of professional development, "handoffs" from one generation to the next, and control over your own destiny.

Now, it may simply be intrinsic to human nature that laurels go to those involved in new client "wins"—it's exciting and newsworthy and the adrenalin and angst that surround any big pitch can ripple far and wide within the firm. Many people probably participate in the pitch, and far more are aware it's going on. Maintaining strong relations with an established client is, simply, less interesting, and certainly not worthy of tallying on a scorecard. Indeed, beyond those working directly with the client, few are probably even aware that anything's going on with the old client at all.

But do we have to encourage new client "origination" so feverishly? With little comparative recognition for building solid, profitable, long-term relationships? (Yes, we're talking about compensation here; I don't mean to be oblique.) In other words, do we need to structurally and affirmatively reinforce what are already—I would argue—shortsighted habits of mind?

We know at least one other thing about client "stickiness." A few years ago Redwood Analytics conducted a study of client attrition across four AmLaw 50 firms over time. The measure of "attrition" could not have been simpler. XYZ was deemed a client during the year if the firm billed them any amount whatsoever; XYZ was not a client if they were not billed at all. Using that unsubtle approach, Redwood determined that the average client attrition rate (in terms of revenue lost) was about 1%/month. Now 1%/month may not sound like so much until you realize it's one-quarter of your revenue every two years.

How to stem that attrition?

Here's the interesting finding:

- The more partners the client interacted with; and

- The more practice groups the client called upon

the less likely they were to fall off the radar. Stated differently, partners (or practice groups) that "hoard" clients for fear of exposing them to other lawyers in the firm are increasing the odds the client will be out the door. Now do you understand why the dreaded "cross-selling" is every marketer's recommendation?

If you want to get serious about an ongoing, structured, consistent approach to enhanced client management, there are some simple, nonthreatening, "Business Development 101" programs out there. We won't get into the weeds on them here and now, but just to take the mystery out of it, the fundamental pieces are:

- Know your client's business

- Know your own firm's capabilities

- Create formal client teams (not ad hoc assemblages for pitches, etc.)

- Have the teams create annual plans, with strategies, action items, quantifiable goals, and evaluative criteria

  - They don't need to be long or elaborate — in fact they should be short and concise — but they need to exist, they need to be clear, and there needs to be accountability for realizing their objectives

- Formalize and institutionalize client feedback

- Deliver "added value" (see above) that clients actually care about. And finally:

- Give meaningful recognition to smart and effective client management at compensation time.

And a final reminder: Why do you want ("need" isn't an exaggeration) to do this?

To avoid becoming an endangered species. Recall the answer to Peter Drucker's question. If that's not motivation enough, good luck.

11: Granting Your Wish

We'll have one more chapter in "Growth is Dead" but let's focus on trying to synthesize a few themes that have been pervasive topics on Adam Smith, Esq., since at least September 15, 2008, and even before, and look at their implications for "Now What?," on the assumption that the thesis of this series has any truth to it.

On Adam Smith, Esq., the recurrent themes include:

- Relentless pricing pressures, which every firm wants to escape from, but only a chosen few will be able to do.

- New, varied, and multiple career paths, with many alternatives to the bimodal partner-track associate or equity partner model.

- Ever accelerating rates of lateral partner mobility.

- And new and/or growing entrants on the landscape, including LPOs, bulked-up inhouse departments, and law firms' own "onshoring" operations.

How do these coalesce in how you should address the "growth is dead" environment?

Well, in the above order, if you want to embrace and turn these trends to your advantage, to "put yourself on the right side of history," as opposed to futile and brittle resistance, rarely a winning game plan, then:

- Discover a way to escape from the vise of pricing pressures by changing the terms of the conversation.

- Prepare to entirely reconceive the demographics of your firm.

- Decide whether the accelerating lateral partner band-wagon can provide enduring value for your firm, or how to do it carefully if it *could* work, or whether to es-chew it, or something else altogether (and remember that this game includes playing defense as well as of-fense).

- Rather than dismissing, or fearing, the new entrants, steal what they do best and jettison what you now do worst.

Got that?

OK, here ends the book.

Just kidding.

Here's another way of thinking about what's happening (although, fair warning, it's offers up no more optimistic prognosis). If we want to trot out Harvard Professor Michael Porter's "Five Forces" Analysis, the fundamental landscape facing BigLaw has become far more challenging in the last few years. Here, in a nutshell, are the five forces that Porter believes shape industry competition and how they've changed in our world recently—every one of the five for the worse, from the perspective of BigLaw:

The Five Forces That Shape Industry Competition

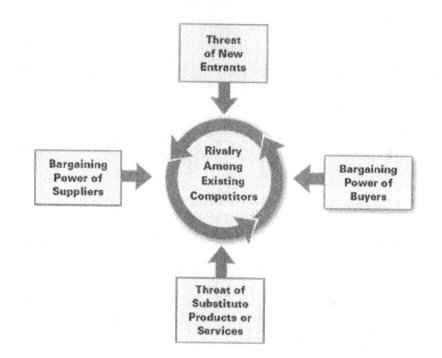

[Graphic courtesy *Harvard Business Review*]

Threat of new competition	High entry barriers are good, as are client loyalty and switching costs	Barriers to entry and switching costs have always been low and if anything, technology is making the costs of starting a new law firm lower than they've ev-

		er been. Now client loyalty is eroding as well
Threat of substitutes	Clients trying substitutes may like what they find and never come back	More substitutes are available, some of them are becoming very good and they'll only get better
Client bargaining power	Price pressures: any questions?	No explanation needed
Bargaining power of suppliers	If "inputs" you can't do without (e.g., talent) have strong leverage over what you must pay them, you will tend to pay what they demand	If anything, the accelerating visibility of superstar laterals potentially puts firms behind the 8-ball
Intensity of competition	The more aggressive (desperate?) your competitors, the more tempted they'll be to engage in irrational behavior	Again, no explanation needed

So much for theory; here's some data (all courtesy of the *Altman Weil 2013 "Law Firms in Transition"* Survey). From 2009 to 2013, the percentage of managing partners believing that these trends are permanent and not cyclical rose as follows:

Yes, Permanent	2009	2013	Increase
More price competition	42.4%	95.6%	2.3X
Fewer equity partners	22.8%	72.1%	3.2X
More contract lawyers	28.3%	74.6%	2.6X
Reduced leverage	12.1%	56.7%	4.7X
More commoditization	25.5%	89.7%	3.5X
Lower PPP	13.2%	55.6%	4.2X
Fewer first year associates	11.4%	62.2%	5.5X
More outsourcing	11.5%	45.5%	4.0X

Note that while the first is explicitly about price (aren't you getting sick of hearing about pricing pressure by now?), the other five are actually all *in response to* pricing pressure. This is what happens to firms when markets shift from the suppliers (that would be us) being price-makers to being price-takers.

Of course, we're not truly "price takers" just yet; we have more than a modicum of control over what we charge. But the tilt of the landscape has indisputably shifted in favor of clients. Let's assume heightened price competition is a given: More than 19 out of 20 managing partners evidently take it as such.

So if the remaining seven trends are responses to pricing pressures, how exactly do they constitute a response and what do they have in common?

I suggest that all seven are ways firms are trying to reconfigure their offerings (read: themselves) to more closely match up with clients' willingness to pay. At the top of the food chain, clients are apparently as willing as ever (more willing?) to pay top dollar for partners who are truly superb, while at the other end of the food chain clients want to pay as little as they can to get their unavoidable commodity-ish work done competently and effectively.

And where does that leave the middle?

Actually, if you have an hypothesis about what happens to the middle, let me know. I'm serious.

Does the client demand function I've been describing remind anyone else of the airline or car industry? — because it does me. Think of partners as Cathay Pacific or Singapore and contract lawyers and outsourcing as Southwest or JetBlue. Or else partners as Audi and BMW and contract lawyers and outsourcing as Toyota and Chevy. The good news is those industries seem to have reached stable equilibria where clients' preferences across a range of quality and service levels and price points are satisfied. The bad news, for traditionalists, is that they bear no resemblance to how we perceive of our profession.

But let's take this thought experiment a step further.

Demographics and Pricing

Do you believe the composition of professionals in your firm, and what you can charge for them, are related? That is to say, that clients more highly value and are willing to pay more for the more highly skilled, experienced partners with quicker and sounder judgment—higher prices than they would pay for anyone else in the firm?

And do you believe that client resentment at paying for all but the most assiduously monitored and metered junior associate time is here to stay?

If you believe those things, which shouldn't require heroic assumptions, then you have to believe that:

- Delivering maximum value to clients, as they perceive it, requires you to change the mix of professionals you deliver;

- Changing the mix of professionals you "deliver" to clients means reconfiguring your firm's own internal mix of professionals, or demographics, as it were;

- And the firm of the future will consist of a much higher ratio of highly valued partners to lower valued associates.

This is not a radical concept, certainly not if you step outside Law Land. (Nor is it by the furthest stretch of the imagination to be taken as critical of associates; they are left virtually defenseless in this economic shift, and if you think I'm callous or indifferent to their fate you haven't heard about my other company.)

Companies reconfigure their product and service offerings all the time, to more closely hew to client demand. It will take us a bit longer, since our "service offerings" consist of professionally trained and highly skilled human beings, but there can be no serious question what the market is calling for. And no one at the level we're talking about wants to work in an organization where their contribution has clearly been marginalized.

So what does this putative firm of the future look like?

For as long as I've been in and around this industry, I have heard *ad* ~~nauseum~~ *infinitum* that firm ABC or XYZ, whether or not they had any remotely plausible aspiration to these leagues, only wants to act on the "highest value," "price-insensitive," "bet the company," "make or break," "premium work."

Your day has arrived. You may wish it hadn't.

Because what is the model I've sketched above? It's a model, as a partner at an AmLaw 10 told me last week, with "clients who are happy to pay $1,100/hour for me but not $400/hour for even a qualified midlevel associate." What is that model?

Wachtell.

We're all Wachtell now, if we can pull it off.

But I put this squarely in the category of "be careful what you wish for," since "being Wachtell" is far more challenging than being a typical AmLaw 50-ish firm—no offense to those of you in that category.

Let's back up: I have a confession. I used "We're all Wachtell now" calculatedly. The phrase—the very mention of the firm's name—can inspire envy in the ranks of those who subscribe to the notion that their firm needs to be in that top right quadrant of the 2 x 2 matrix, the "highest value," "premium work," etc., engagements. And of course, who can object to Wachtell staking out its own party-of-one place in the PEP stratosphere?

But that's not all the Wachtell model is about. There are two other critical elements more challenging to embrace: (1) that 1:1 partner:associate leverage, and (2) their intense focus on highly specialized and narrow lines of business, without deviation.

Achieving (1) is going to require wrenching changes in almost every firm that chooses to go down that path, and it can risk introducing centrifugal forces that can tear the place apart before you can achieve the goal.

And as for (2), it requires saying No relentlessly, and many more times than you'll ever get to say Yes.

Are you game?

And if not, what's your plan?

We'll have some final thoughts on that.

12: THE S-CURVE

As we come to the final chapter of Growth is Dead, I hope the challenge I've laid out for us is clear.

- Excess capacity

- Stagnant demand

- Cut-throat or "suicidal" discounting

- Unprecedented pressure on prices, from all directions, including who clients will pay for, and rates and realization

- Exhaustion of cost-cutting as a tactic to keep profit margins intact

Among other things, I've suggested the new landscape will require:

- Law firms to restructure their "demographics" in profound ways, from pyramids to cylinders

    o And far savvier and nimble readiness to draw upon "the cloud" of virtually available talent, be it alumni networks, your own onshoring operations, or even third parties

    o (Think of all of this as just-in-time supply)

- Astute, targeted, **knowing** focus on clients' businesses so that they come to see you as partners in solving their problems and not the "outside counsel vendor"

- Willingness to invest for the long run and not feel compelled to strip-mine the balance sheet of cash within
  weeks of the conclusion of each fiscal year

Note that last point.

My greatest fear for the industry at this juncture is that short-term imperatives will override sound judgment and prudence, and that a few firms may be tempted not only to short-change the long run but to mortgage tomorrow to juice up today. I for one do not presume we're too smart to know better; why should we be? Dewey beyond a reasonable doubt did it, and whether or not you personally believe them to be an outlier, governments, financial institutions, corporations, and households around the world were (we know now) doing it throughout the first decade of this century. I would not be shocked were some law firms to fall into the same beguiling trap.

But that's actually for another day.

Let's put this into larger historical perspective.

Industries tend to follow quasi-biological life cycles of birth (invention/creation), childhood (halting steps), adolescence (self-discovery), rapid acceleration into maturity and supremely competent adulthood (what in ecology would be called the "climax phase") and, yes, senescence and decline.

In terms of Law Land, a rough analogy is that Paul Cravath's invention of his System a century or so ago represented our passage beyond childhood into adolescence, and that it's all been one long, extended, increasingly glorious adulthood ever since, as we've refined and tweaked and buffed the model around the edges, making no material changes.

And boy, did it ever deliver the goods, in terms of BigLaw growing as a share of GDP and PPP growing in relation to the average worker's earnings. And it worked for virtually everyone who'd climbed aboard the bus, whether they were terribly introspective and astute about what they were doing or not. Until about 2008, that is.

Now we're in a transition phase, I believe, where a tremendous premium will be placed on firms' ability to figure out their rightful place in this world, and clear blue water will begin to appear between firms who go on to ever greater strength and those who find themselves relatively marginalized and, yes, irrelevant.

We are scarcely the first, nor will we be the last, industry to go through this life cycle.

Indeed, this life cycle is so well-known that it has been diagrammed, and it's called the "S-Curve." Here it is:

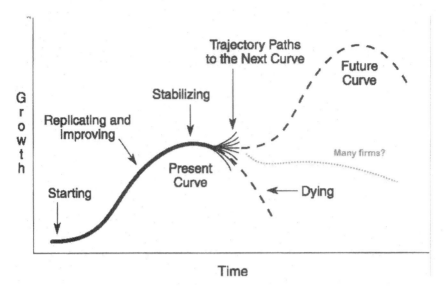

(Image courtesy CEO ThinkTank.)

I submit we may be approaching the fraying ends of the "Present Curve," where the "Next Curve" is indistinctly and dimly not quite yet in focus.

What determines the speed with which clients adopt the "next curve?" Three primary factors, none of which bodes well for those wedded to the status quo:

- Relative superiority: How much better is the new than the old? Many clients seem to think the old is not great.

- Complexity vs. simplicity: Is the new difficult to use or adopt? Given that clients are largely driving it, I'd have to guess not.

- Awareness: If no one has ever heard of the "next thing," good luck with it. Everyone has heard of LPO's, alternative fees, etc.

To be clear: I do not envision this as the phase-jump from circuit boards to microchips, analog to digital, or CRT to flat-panel, where the original incumbent was supplanted in its entirety. No. Law firms as we know them are not going away.

Rather, I see this as a jump from a world where merely to BE a conventional law firm was to live at the climax stage of the "Present Curve," into a world where performance of some firms will vault onto the "Future Curve," while that of others (most?) will follow the irresolute trajectory I've depicted with the dotted line labeled "Many firms?"

Why, you might be asking yourself, would any rational firm choose—and it is a choice—to stick with the declining model?

Now, this may not be an answer, but it's a reality: Firms in every industry do this all the time. Perhaps the most well-known recent excavation into how this happens was Clayton Christensen's THE INNOVATOR'S DILEMMA but I recently discovered an even earlier and at least as nuanced a treatment of the phenomenon in Peter Drucker's Innovation and Entrepreneurship (1985). The following excerpts are from his chapters on "Industry & Market Structures" (pp. 76 et seq.) (all emphasis mine).

> Industry and market structures sometimes last for many, many years and seem completely stable. ... Indeed, industry and market structures appears so solid that the people in an industry are likely to consider them foreordained, part of the order of nature, and certain to endure forever.

> Actually, market and industry structures are quite brittle ...

In industry structure, a change requires entrepreneurship from every member of the industry. It requires that each one ask anew: "What is our business?" And **each of the members will have to give a different, but above all a new, answer** to that question.

...

A change in industry structure offers exceptional opportunities, highly visible and quite predictable to outsider. But the insiders perceive these same changes primarily as threats. The outsiders who innovate can thus become a major factor in an important industry or area quite fast, and at relatively low risk.

Drucker also identifies "near-certain, highly visible indicators of impending change in industry structure," which include:

- Rapid growth and the success of existing practices, "so nobody is inclined to tamper with them" despite their becoming obsolete;

- A tendency to become complacent and above all to "skim the cream;"

- A tendency to define and analyze the market based on history and not reality.

And this from "Hit Them Where They Ain't" (pp. 220 et seq.):

Some fairly common bad habits that enable newcomers to use entrepreneurial judo and to catapult themselves into a leadership position in an industry against the entrenched, established companies:

1. "NIH," or not invented here; because we didn't think of it, it can't be of great value;

2. Again, the tendency to "cream" a market, that is to get the high-profit part of it, which is always punished by loss of market and trying to get paid for past rather than current contributions;

3. Even more debilitating, according to Drucker, is the third bad habit: the belief in "quality." "Quality" in a product or service is not what the supplier puts in. It is what the customer gets out and is willing to pay for. A product is not "quality" because it is hard to make and costs a lot of money; that is incompetence. Customers pay only for what is of use to them and gives them value. Nothing else constitutes "quality."

4. The delusion of the "premium" price. A "premium" price is always an invitation to the competitor.

Harsh words, harsh advice? Indeed.

Yet firms once upon a time as distinguished as RCA, Xerox, Bell Labs, US Steel, Westinghouse, Kodak, Honeywell, and countless others have failed to learn these lessons at their peril.

This is not the type of history we should want to repeat. So what now?

Plenty of folks are happy to tell you (for a fine sum) that the answer is (pick one):

- (a) to get global, and fast, preferably by merging on payment of a "success" fee;

- (b) to adopt a single-minded laser focus on what you do best;

- (c) to double down on client service;

- (d) to go the boutique route;

- (e) to become an exquisitely talented maestro of assembling just-in-time teams you put together for one project at a time, with the precise blend of talents, capabilities, and capacities to get the job done and then to disperse (think producing a Hollywood movie or constructing a major downtown office building);

- (f) to relentlessly pursue the top right quadrant of that handy two-by-two matrix and spurn all but the most high value, premium, price-insensitive work (this is a perennial entrant in the strategy race);

- (g) and surely there are other configurations I've missed.

My own idea is somewhat different.

We have no idea yet what BigLaw (or more accurately, SophisticatedLaw) will look like in the future, and **the only way to find out is to invent that future.**

Please take this as a gravely serious observation, not flippant or glib in the least.

Remember what Drucker said about each firm having to find its own (new) answer as to what it's business is. Time for creativity, imagination, innovation. Try things. But don't try one big thing, try lots of little things. Don't put all your chips in the center of the table; learn as you go along, make midcourse corrections, seek continuous feedback, react. As Air Force fighter pilots have been taught since the days of the Korean War, in a dogfight you have to observe the "OODA" loop:

- Observe your environment;

- Orient yourselves towards your clients and competitors;

- Decide what you're going to do RIGHT NOW;

- Act

- (Repeat)

Grand plans don't perform well in midair, and it may feel to some of us as if we're being thrown into midair. Nimbleness, decisiveness, and immediate readjustment perform much better. Lawyers' problem is we don't do nimble well.

Step back: Imagine someone presenting you 10 years ago with a slim plastic/metal slab slightly longer, narrower, and much slimmer than a pack of cards and asking you what you would like such a device to do if you could carry it around in your pocket or purse all day long? I suspect most of us—most assuredly including yours truly—would have had not the remotest idea. Tell time? Play music?

Or, far more historically profound, recall your high school or college biology and learning about the Cambrian Explosion. Some 650 million years ago life on Earth changed in ways never seen before or since: All the major phyla and forms of animals we know today suddenly appeared; we went from "almost nothing to almost everything, almost overnight," as one biologist put it.

Two critical points: First, no one saw it coming (assuming the counterfactual that there had been anyone to observe it beforehand); and second, it involved wildly unbridled trial and error, with far more extinctions than successes. Yet the successes were world class: Limbs for locomotion, eyes and ears, digestive and reproductive systems and the start of organized neural networks to mastermind it all.

I think we may be at a similar turning point. It's time to experiment, folks, to learn from what fails and what succeeds, and to invent our futures, even though we have no idea what it will look like yet. This is not optional; it is the signal challenge confronting us. It's not too much to say that if we don't get this right, nothing else matters.

Because if we don't do this, someone else is going to do it for us and to us.

Let's get to work.

ABOUT THE AUTHOR

Bruce MacEwen is a lawyer and consultant to law firms on strategic and economic issues, Bruce is President of Adam Smith, Esq. (AdamSmithEsq.com), an online publication providing insights on the economics and business of law firms. The site enjoys a worldwide readership, and since its launch in late 2003, Bruce has published nearly 1,500 articles, covering such topics as strategy, leadership, globalization, M&A, finance, compensation, cultural considerations, and partnership structures.

Adam Smith, Esq. is also a management consultancy to law firms and the legal industry.

Bruce has written for or been quoted in: *Fortune; The Wall Street Journal; The New York Times; The Washington Post; Bloomberg News/Radio/TV; Business 2.0; The International Herald Tribune; The National Law Journal; The ABA Journal; The Lawyer;* and other publications too numerous to mention. He is a sought-after speaker and frequently appears at law firm retreats and legal industry conferences domestically and overseas.

Bruce is a Fellow in the College of Law Practice Management, "formed to honor and recognize distinguished law practice management professionals [and to] inspire excellence and innovation by honoring extraordinary achievement."

Previously, Bruce:

- Practiced securities law in-house for nearly ten years at Morgan Stanley/Dean Witter; and
- Practiced litigation and corporate law with Shea & Gould and with Breed, Abbott & Morgan in New York.

Bruce was educated at Princeton University (BA *magna cum laude* in economics), at Stanford Law School (JD), and at NYU's Stern School of Business (MBA candidate in finance).

A native Manhattanite, he lives on New York's Upper West Side with his wife and their dog.

GROWTH IS DEAD SEMINARS

Adam Smith, Esq. offers seminars addressing the issues raised by *Growth is Dead* customized to the particular circumstances of your firm. Contact Bruce to learn more.

NOTES

Made in the USA
Charleston, SC
26 January 2015